D1100300

STENDHAL

The Red and the Black

Retold by F. H. Cornish

Book sale

MACMILLAN

Fo...

Macmillan Readers p...
for learners of Engli...
Starter, Beginner, Ele...
Upper.

Level control

Information, structure and vocabulary are controlled to suit the students' ability at each level.

The number of words at each level:

Starter	about 300 basic words
Beginner	about 600 basic words
Elementary	about 1100 basic words
Pre-intermediate	about 1400 basic words
Intermediate	about 1600 basic words
Upper	about 2200 basic words

Vocabulary

Some difficult words and phrases in this book are important for understanding the story. Some of these words are explained in the story and some are shown in the pictures. From Pre-Intermediate level upwards, words are marked with a number like this: ...[3]. These words are explained in the Glossary at the end of the book.

Answer key

An Answer key for the *Points for Understanding* section can be found at www.macmillanenglish.com/readers

Contents

Notes About the Author and France Between 1783 and 1842

Stendhal was the name used by the French writer, Marie-Henri Beyle. Henri Beyle liked to use false names instead of his true name.

Stendhal was a clever man who liked to tell jokes. He enjoyed making people laugh. But he was also shy – he felt uncomfortable when he met strangers and he could not talk to them easily.

Stendhal did many different kinds of work during his life. He was a merchant, a soldier, a diplomat[1] and a writer. But he never had much money. When he had money, he spent it on fashionable clothes and good food and drink. Stendhal fell in love with many women, but he never married.

Stendhal was born in Grenoble in France, on 23rd January 1783. When he was seven years old, Stendhal's mother died. He did not have a good relationship[2] with his father and they often quarrelled[3]. When he was a young boy, Stendhal was educated in his home. His teachers were priests[4]. Between 1796 and 1799, Stendhal attended a school in Grenoble. He was a good student of mathematics and he enjoyed reading the poems and plays of William Shakespeare.

Many changes took place in France when Stendhal was a child. King Louis XVI[5] ruled France from 1774 to 1792. The king and his family lived in large and beautiful palaces and they spent a lot of money. Louis chose the ministers of his government and he made all the important decisions about his country.

There were three classes – or levels – of society in France. These classes were called the First Estate, the Second Estate and the Third Estate. The people of the First Estate were important members of the Church. For example, bishops,

4

archbishops and cardinals. Members of the First Estate did not have to pay much tax[6] and they did not have to fight for their country. They owned about 20% of the land.

The highest class of society was the Second Estate. The members of this class were aristocrats[7]. Members of these rich, powerful families had served[8] the rulers of France for many hundreds of years. Aristocrats often became ministers in the government and some of them lived and worked in the palaces of the royal family. Many aristocrats were soldiers of high rank[9] who fought battles[10] for their country. They often received money and honours[11] from the king. Aristocrats owned about 33% of the land and they did not have to pay much tax to the government.

The Third Estate contained poor, low-class people and middle-class people. Businessmen and professionals such as lawyers, doctors, bankers and teachers were members of the Third Estate. Poor priests, merchants and peasants[12] were also members of the Third Estate. People in this level of society could not become ministers in the government. They had to pay the largest amount of tax. About 80% of the French people were peasants. The peasants' lives were very difficult. Very few of them owned the land where they worked. Peasants had to pay money to the government, to the Church, and to the owners of their land. Peasants also had to fight in wars.

When King Louis XVI needed money, he tried to make the landowners pay him more money. So the landowners made the peasants on their land pay them more money. After this, the members of the Third Estate started to ask for power. They wanted to say how France should be governed. They spoke out about this to the king and his officials. The peasants and the workers of France became more and more unhappy.

In 1788 there was very little food in France. Thousands of peasants were very hungry. On 14th July 1789, a crowd attacked the Bastille prison in Paris. They killed the governor of the prison and released the prisoners. This was the beginning of the French Revolution.

By September 1792, the people of France had decided that they no longer wanted a king to rule them. The people wanted to rule their own country. They wanted France to be a republic. In December 1792, Louis XVI was taken to a court. At his trial, Louis was accused of being a traitor[13] and on 21st January 1793, he was executed[14]. After this, a group of people called Jacobins[15] controlled France. Anyone who spoke against the new republican leaders was executed.

Between 1793 and 1795 a great number of French people were put into prisons. Very few of these prisoners had a trial in a court before they were executed. Almost every French aristocrat was killed. Their heads cut off by guillotines[16].

In 1793, a young French soldier became famous while the French army was fighting a war against Britain. The young man, who came from a poor family, was the son of a lawyer. His name was Napoleon Bonaparte. Napoleon was so successful that by 1796, he had become the leader of the French army.

Stendhal quarrelled with his father in 1799 and he went to live in Paris. He became a diplomat and worked for the French Ministry of War.

In September 1800, Stendhal travelled to Italy and joined Napoleon Bonaparte's Army of Italy. Stendhal did not know how to fight – he had not trained to be a soldier. But he was given the rank of sub-lieutenant.

He had to write reports about the fighting and send them to the Ministry of War. Stendhal was not a soldier for very long. He became ill in 1801 and had to return to Paris.

From 1802 to 1806, Stendhal was a merchant and he

worked for the French government. He travelled between France and Italy many times. While he was in Italy, he fell in love with a woman called Angela Pietragrua.

Napoleon became Emperor of France in 1804. This was a powerful position. He controlled armies, the government and the money. At this time, many countries in western Europe became part of the French Empire. And during Napoleon Bonaparte's rule there were new ideas about art, fashion, literature, architecture, education and government.

From 1812 to 1814, Napoleon's armies fought battles in Russia, Germany, Austria and Spain. But by the spring of 1814, Napoleon's armies had become weak. Napoleon lost several important battles and there were not enough soldiers to protect[17] France from the armies of its enemies. By the first week in May 1814, Napoleon was no longer Emperor of France. He was sent to live on the island of Elba, in the Mediterranean Sea.

On 3rd May 1814, Louis XVIII, the brother of Louis XVI, became King of France. Louis XVIII was not a popular king and many people wanted Napoleon to be their ruler again.

Napoleon escaped from Elba on 1st March 1815,and he went to Paris. He became Emperor once more, but he only ruled for one hundred days. His enemies, called Ultras[18], wanted a king to rule the country. On 14th June 1815, Napoleon's army fought at the Battle of Waterloo. But Napoleon lost the battle and he was sent to a prison on the island of Saint Helena. He died there in 1821.

In 1820, Stendhal had to leave Italy because officials of the Italian government thought that he was a spy[19]. Stendhal went to live in Paris.

After Napoleon lost the Battle of Waterloo, Louis XVIII became king again. When Louis died, his brother Charles was king from 1824 to 1830.

Stendhal wrote his novel *The Red and the Black* in 1829.

His story shows how life in France changed after Napoleon was defeated and France had a king again. Stendhal uses the character, Julien Sorel, to show how much dishonesty and corruption[20] there was in France at this time.

In July 1830, Louis-Philippe I became King of France. *The Red and the Black* was published in November of the same year. Stendhal was in Italy at this time. He lived near Rome. He wanted to marry a young Italian woman called Giulia Rinieri. But Giulia's family told Stendhal that he could not marry her.

Between 1831 and 1837, Stendhal started writing many different stories, plays and essays but he finished very few of them. In 1835, he was awarded the Cross of the Legion of Honour for his diplomatic work. Stendhal wrote four novels and about twelve short stories. He wrote books about art, music, literature and philosophy. And he wrote about the lives of musicians, painters and poets.

In 1838, Stendhal met Giulia Rinieri again. Soon after this, he began another novel, *The Charterhouse of Parma*. He finished writing the book in seven weeks. It was published in April 1839, when Stendhal was fifty-six years old.

In 1840, Stendhal met Giulia Rinieri in Florence, in Italy. It was the last time that he saw her. By 1841, Stendhal had become ill and lonely. He returned to Paris and on 22nd March 1842, he fell in the street. He died the next morning. Stendhal's body was taken to Paris and buried[21] in a tomb in Montmartre.

The People and Places in This Story

Monsieur – Mr, or Sir. (abbreviation = M.)

Madame – Mrs, or Madam. (abbreviation = Mme)

Mademoiselle – Miss, a young or unmarried woman. (abbreviation = Mlle)

Marquis – an aristocrat. The full name would be given as 'Monsieur, the Marquis X'.

Marquise – an aristocrat, the wife of a marquis. The full name would be given as 'Madame, the Marquise X'.

Comte – an aristocrat. A count was the son of a marquis. The full name would be given as 'Monsieur, the Comte X'.

Monseigneur – the title used for a bishop, who was an important priest of the Catholic Church in France. e.g. Monseigneur, the Bishop of X.

M. de La Mole	*Curé Chélan*
M. de Rênal	*Abbé Pirard*
M. Valenod	*Abbé Chas-Bernard*
Fouqué	*Élisa*

France was divided into large areas called *régions*. Each région contained areas called *départements*. In each département, there were smaller areas called *communes*. Each commune had a group of towns and villages that were led by a *mayor*.

Most of this story takes place in the département called Franche-Comté, which is in the eastern part of France, near Switzerland.

On the eastern side of Franche-Comté, are the Jura Mountains. The largest river in this area is the River Doubs. The towns and cities of Besançon, Grenoble, Mainz, Metz and Paris are real places.

But in this story, the villages of Verrières and Vergy are not real places.

9

Verrières

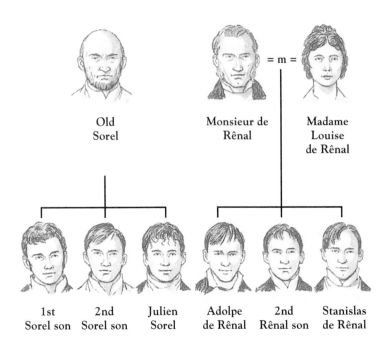

Old
Sorel

Monsieur de
Rênal

= m =

Madame
Louise
de Rênal

1st
Sorel son

2nd
Sorel son

Julien
Sorel

Adolpe
de Rênal

2nd
Rênal son

Stanislas
de Rênal

Monsieur
Valenod

Fouqué

Curé
Chélan

The King
of —

The Bishop
of Agde

Vergy

Élisa

Madame
Derville

Paris

 = m =

Marquis
de La Mole

Marquise
de La Mole

Besançon

Abbé Pirard

Abbé
Chas-Bernard

Norbert,
Comte de La
Mole

Mathilde,
Mademoiselle
de La Mole

Metz

Prince X

The Italian
Jansenist

11

1

The Mayor and the Peasant's Son

The town of Verrières is in the eastern part of France
which is called Franche-Comté. Verrières is close to the
Jura Mountains and the border[22] with Switzerland. The
pretty little town stands beside the River Doubs. The
roofs of the white houses are covered with red tiles and tall
chestnut trees grow along the sides of the streets.

The people of Verrières worked hard and they lived
happily and well. There were several sawmills[23] in the
town and many of the townspeople earned money by
preparing timber from the trees which grew on the
mountains. These timber merchants cut down the trees
and made wooden boards from the timber. Then they sold
the boards to builders and people who made furniture.
Other townspeople earned money by preparing a special
kind of strong, coloured cloth. And Verrières also had one
modern business – a nail factory. In this factory, the water
from the River Doubs was used to drive huge mechanical
hammers. The heavy, noisy hammers made small pieces of
iron into sharp nails. Builders used the nails to join pieces
of timber together.

The nail factory was owned by Monsieur de Rênal – the
richest and most important man in Verrières. The Rênal
family had lived in the town for more than two hundred
years. M. de Rênal's father, grandfather and great-grandfather
had all lived and worked in Verrières. They had all made
and sold iron products.

In the autumn of 1815, the people of the town made M.
de Rênal their leader. He became the mayor of Verrières.

1815 was an especially happy year for M. de Rênal

because there was a king ruling France again. Rênal was an Ultra. He believed that France should be ruled by a king. He had hated everything about the Revolution. He had hated the Jacobins, and everything that they had done. He had hated Napoleon Bonaparte and his Empire. And now that there was a king again, Rênal hated anyone who wanted to change society in any way. He hated all Liberals[24]!

When he became the mayor of Verrières, M. de Rênal wanted everyone to forget that he owned the nail factory. He only wanted them to think of him as an important official. Why? Because things like factories were *modern*. Whenever people thought about modern things and the changes in the world – they also thought about things like the Revolution and the Bonapartists. Rênal was not a modern man. But he was a proud man and he wanted to be respected[25].

In small towns like Verrières, everyone thought about money. They wanted to earn money and keep it. People in small towns respected anyone who was rich. And a good way to become rich was to buy land. Everyone respected people who had money and land. Middle-class people bought land next to their houses and extended the size of their gardens. Then they built high walls around their gardens.

A fine house, with a large garden and high walls, would always impress[26] your friends and the people who lived near you. If you had these things, your friends and neighbours would call you a 'landowner'. They would not say that you were a factory-owner. So, in 1821, Rênal started to extend his garden and to build walls. But he soon had a problem.

The mayor's problem came from a clever peasant called Sorel. Sorel was an old man with three sons. He owned a sawmill on land which was beside Rênal's garden wall. The mayor now wanted this land to extend his garden. But it was not easy to make deals with[27] the clever old peasant. At last, Rênal got the extra land for his garden, but the deal was

13

expensive. First, old Sorel wanted a large piece of land that belonged to Rênal's family. Sorel was going to build a new sawmill on this piece of land, which was next to the river. Then Sorel wanted a large sum of money.

Rênal knew that the piece of land next to the river was a much better place for Sorel's business. Sorel could use the water from the river to drive his saws which cut the timber. And his business would be in a position which was closer to the centre of the town.

For these reasons, Rênal was angry about the deal that Sorel wanted. But there was nothing that the mayor could do about it. So, in 1821, he made the agreement with old Sorel and he extended his garden. But after that, whenever he saw the old peasant and his growing sons, Rênal's thoughts were dark and angry.

The mayor had no reason to like the Sorel family. However, on the day when this story really begins, he made a strange decision. On that fine autumn day in 1826, he decided to invite Julien Sorel – the old peasant's youngest son – to live in his house. The mayor wanted the young man to live in his home and teach his three children.

Why did Rênal make this decision? He did it because he wanted to impress his neighbours. His neighbours did not have tutors for *their* children. And they knew that it was expensive to employ a tutor. Why did Rênal choose Julien Sorel for the job? Well, he knew that Julien was clever. If Rênal did not employ the young man as *his* family tutor, one of his *neighbours* would soon employ him. Also, Rênal knew that Julien had been studying theology[28] because he wanted to become a priest.

'People who want to be priests are never Bonapartists or Jacobins,' thought Rênal. 'Everyone knows that Bonapartists and Jacobins hate the Church.'

Rênal went and spoke to his wife.

14

Rênal was angry about the deal that Sorel wanted. But there was nothing that the mayor could do about it.

'Young Sorel knows Latin[29],' Rênal said, 'so he can't be a Liberal. Liberals don't study Latin. Yes, I've decided. Old Sorel's youngest son must come to live with us. Julien Sorel must teach our children. I'll speak to his father about it today.'

'Yes, it's a good idea,' Madame Louise de Rênal said.

She did not quarrel with her husband about this plan. She was a calm and beautiful thirty-year-old woman – about twenty years younger than her husband.

Madame de Rênal did not enjoy the company of most people in Verrières. She thought that most people in Verrières were noisy and bad-mannered[30]. She disliked the way that they thought only about money. But she admired[31] her husband. He was planning for their children's future and she admired this.

The Rênals had three children – all sons. The oldest boy, Adolphe, was only eleven years old. But M. de Rênal had already planned all his children's careers[32]. So Mme de Rênal was happy when she heard the news about the tutor.

Madame de Rênal was fond of her husband – she liked and cared for him very much because she knew him well. But she did not love him. In fact, she was a little bored with him. But she did not want to think about this.

2

The New Tutor

Julien Sorel was a slim young man of medium height – he was not too short or too tall. He had pale skin, long red-brown hair, and large dark eyes. He was about nineteen years old, but he looked much younger. Julien was a very handsome young man and the women of Verrières had started to notice[33] his good looks.

Julien's father and his older brothers hated him. They were all tall strong men and they worked hard in the sawmill. But they were not well-educated or intelligent.

Julien was not very strong, and he was not interested in the sawmill. He read books about religion, and he studied the poems of classical Greek and Roman authors. So when Rênal asked old Sorel if he could take Julien away from the sawmill, the clever peasant was pleased.

But Sorel did not show the mayor that he was pleased. And he did not agree immediately to the mayor's offer. Old Sorel pretended[34] that another rich man also wanted to employ his son. But when Rênal offered to buy new clothes for Julien, and pay him four hundred francs a year, old Sorel agreed.

As soon as the mayor had left the sawmill, old Sorel went to find Julien. He found his son sitting near the mechanical saw. But Julien was not watching the sharp saw as it cut the timber. The young man was reading his favourite book – a book about Napoleon. The old peasant did not know this because he could not read. Because he could not read himself, he did not understand why his son had wanted to learn this skill.

'The boy certainly doesn't have any *useful* skills,' the old man thought. 'He's useless in the sawmill. He reads books and dreams all day.' And these thoughts made the old man angry.

'You're no use to us here, boy!' old Sorel shouted at Julien. 'Someone else wants to employ you and this sawmill will be better without you. In the morning, you can pack your bag and go!'

Julien Sorel was unlike his father and his brothers in another way. All his ideas about the world came from books. Julien had only a few books and he had loved them for many years. When Julien was a young boy, an old man had taught him to read. This old man had been a doctor in Napoleon's army. The doctor had taught Julien some Latin and some French history. And he had also taught Julien to think, and to make decisions. For many years, the old doctor was Julien's best friend. When the doctor died, Julien received a little money from him, as well as all of his books.

Many of the doctor's books were about liberal politics and about the Emperor Napoleon. Perhaps if Rênal had known this, he would not have employed Julien. But Rênal did not know this. He only knew that Julien was a scholar[35] of Latin. The mayor wanted his own children to learn Latin.

Julien had studied Latin because he hated his life in the sawmill. He wanted to leave the sawmill and become a priest. Julien believed that if he became a priest, he would improve his life. He would become rich and successful. Priests had to be able to read and understand Latin. The language used in churches was Latin. And many religious books were written in Latin. The old doctor had started to teach Julien Latin, and now the priest of Verrières – Curé Chélan – was teaching Julien a lot more.

When he was a young boy, Julien had wanted to become a soldier. He had wanted to wear a beautiful red uniform and fight battles. He wanted money and power. He wanted to be like his hero[36], Napoleon Bonaparte. Julien knew that Napoleon's family had been poor – like his own family. Napoleon had started his own career as a simple soldier. By the time that he was twenty-seven years old, Napoleon had become the leader of the French army. Then he had become Emperor of France and ruler of much of Europe. But now France had a king again.

'The priests have all the power in this country now,' Julien thought. 'I'll become a priest and wear black clothes. I'll show people that I'm intelligent and well-educated. People will respect me. Then perhaps I'll be powerful and successful.'

Julien was clever and he had a very good memory. He learned things easily and he remembered them. He quickly became a very good Latin scholar. Julien wanted Curé Chélan's help. So he decided to impress the kind old priest and show him that he was a good student. Julien learned by heart[37] the whole of the New Testament of the Bible. Because his memory was so good, Julien found this easy. The curé *had* been very impressed and he had agreed to teach Julien theology. Curé Chélan did not know that Julien had no belief in God or the Bible. He did not know that Julien was only interested in improving his life. And the young man did not tell the old priest this, of course.

———

It was the morning of the first day of Julien Sorel's new life. Today, he was going to begin his job as the tutor to the mayor's children. Julien was going to live with the Rênal family and eat all his meals with them. He would be like a member of the mayor's family.

It was a difficult morning for Madame Louise de Rênal. She had spoken to her servants and made arrangements for the new tutor. Julien was going to have a good room in the mayor's fine house. The servants had moved the beds of the Rênals' three young sons into this room. Julien was going to be with the boys all the time. From today, he was going to look after them and teach them to behave well.

Louise de Rênal was sad and worried.

'Perhaps this new tutor will be cruel to my boys,' she thought. 'Perhaps he'll punish[38] my dear sons without good reasons. But I won't be able to help them. From today, I won't be alone with them very often.'

Louise was thinking these unhappy thoughts while she stood in her sitting-room. This room had tall windows which looked onto the Rênals' beautiful large garden.

When she stepped out of one of these windows and into the garden, she saw a slim, pale man standing in front of the house. He looked very young – little more than a boy. Louise watched him. He was trying to find the courage[39] to ring the bell beside the front door.

'Who is this young man?' Louise asked herself. 'He must have come to talk about business with my husband. But he looks terrified.'

Louise walked towards the nervous young man.

'Can I help you, monsieur?' she asked. 'Who are you looking for here?'

Surprised by her voice, Julien Sorel turned round and looked at the woman. He was amazed by her beauty. For a few moments, he was unable to speak. Louise had to repeat her question.

'I–I've come to see the mayor, madame,' Julien replied. 'I have a job – a position – here. I'm the tutor.' His cheeks became red and he looked at the ground.

Louise was suddenly very happy. She had expected the tutor to be an older man. She had been expecting a cruel man who would make her boys unhappy. And now she saw this shy boy who had pale skin, large eyes and long, curling hair. This beautiful person had come to teach her boys Latin! Now she knew that she had nothing to fear.

'I hope that you'll be kind to my sons, monsieur,' she said gently.

Until that morning, Julien had lived the life of a peasant. He could not believe what he was hearing. Nobody had ever called him 'monsieur' before! No one had spoken to him so politely. And now he had been called 'monsieur' twice by this very beautiful woman. In a moment, there were tears on his cheeks.

Louise de Rênal saw Julien's tears and her happiness increased. She liked shy people because she was a shy person

The young man suddenly held her hand and kissed it.

herself. She asked Julien to follow her into the house. And when the young man suddenly held her hand and kissed it, she did not complain[40]. But she was certainly very surprised!

'He's only a boy,' Louise told herself. 'He does things before he thinks.'

When Julien kissed Louise de Rênal's hand, it was an important moment in her life. But Louise did not understand this at the time. She did not know Julien Sorel. She did not know that he always thought before he did things. She was impressed by him. Julien had kissed her hand because he thought that this was the correct way to behave. He only knew this: Men who were called by the name 'monsieur' had good manners. They bowed their heads politely when they greeted men. They kissed women's hands when they met them. Julien had read about these things in books. But the books were old and Julien had never met anyone from the middle-class before.

Julien wanted to be rich, successful and important. He had left the home of his lower-class, peasant family. He was now going to live in the home of the mayor. He had taken his first step up into middle-class society. From now, Julien would always do what he thought would be good for *him*. He was not interested in sincerity[41]. From now, he would say what people wanted to hear. Julien was like an actor. He was always thinking about other peoples' opinions[42] of him. But he did not know this – he had never seen an actor.

––––––

Later that day, Monsieur de Rênal took Julien to a tailor[43]. The tailor was going to make a suit of black clothes for Julien. When they returned to the house, the mayor introduced his three sons to their new tutor. Julien spoke kindly to them and showed them his Bible.

'I'm here to teach you Latin,' Julien told the boys. 'Together, we'll study this book. It is the story of the life of

Jesus – and it's written in Latin. It will be your guide for the whole of your lives.'

'When we study our lessons,' Julien went on. 'I'll often test your knowledge[44] of this book. But first, you must test my knowledge of it.'

He gave the book to the oldest boy, Adolphe.

'Open the book at any page,' Julien said. 'Read the first few words. Then I'll continue.'

Adolphe de Rênal opened the book and read a few words. Julien immediately remembered this part of the Bible. He remembered every word on the page and recited[45] them. This happened again and again. Adolphe opened the book in many different places. Each time, he read a few words on a page. Then Julien recited the rest of the words on each page.

The Rênals were amazed by Julien's skill. The servants heard Julien and they were amazed. Then Adolphe's two brothers tested Julien's knowledge. The young scholar did not make one mistake.

In the evening, several of the mayor's neighbours visited the house. Julien's skill was shown to them too. They were all very impressed. Rênal was a very happy man.

3

Madame de Rênal

After a few weeks, Julien seemed happy and confident[46] in the mayor's house. Everybody called him 'monsieur', and this pleased him. But Julien could not forget his peasant family and he could not forget the liberal politics that he had learned from the old doctor. Julien did not really like the mayor's young sons, but no one guessed this. The young man taught the boys well and they all liked him – in fact, they adored[47] him.

All the time that Julien worked in the Rênals' house, the tutor never showed his real feelings. The young man was polite and quiet. He read his Bible for many hours each day. No one guessed that Julien did not believe the words that he read there. If anybody talked about Napoleon Bonaparte, Julien was always angry and scornful[48]. But the truth was this: Julien admired Napoleon and he hated the rich, middle-class people who he now met every day. Poor peasants like the Sorel family had always been treated with contempt[49] by middle-class people.

Whenever Rênal or one of his rich friends talked about politics, Julien was silent and angry.

'The mayor and his friends are all Ultras!' the young tutor thought.

Julien strongly disagreed with the opinions of the mayor and his friends, but he could not say this. Julien needed his job. So he pretended to admire Rênal. And he pretended to respect Rênal's opinions.

Julien often thought that the mayor and his friends were wrong, even though he did not understand what they were talking about. Julien had knowledge of only a few subjects. And he certainly did not know about life outside the small town of Verrières. Julien knew about theology, which he had studied with Curé Chélan. And he knew Latin, because the curé and the old doctor had taught him the language. But apart from Latin, the old doctor had talked about only two subjects. These subjects were the battles which Napoleon's army had fought, and soldiers' injuries and illnesses. Of course, the conversations in the mayor's house were never about these subjects.

At first, Julien Sorel's new life was not very different from his old life. He was living with people that he secretly hated and who secretly hated him. Rênal and his friends treated the young tutor with contempt. When Julien had lived with his father and brothers, they had treated him with contempt too. But they had told Julien that they hated him. They had not kept their feelings hidden. However, Julien realized that there was one person in the mayor's house who did not hate him. And that person was Madame de Rênal. She did not hate him or treat him with contempt. In fact, the more time that Mme de Rênal was with the young tutor, the more she liked him.

Louise de Rênal saw how her husband treated the young tutor and she disliked this. She tried to help Julien. She gave him money for some new shirts. But he was proud and he would not accept this gift.

'I will *not* be treated like a servant, madame,' he told her coldly. His words made Louise like and respect Julien more. But when she repeated his words to her husband, the mayor laughed.

'Of course I'll treat him like a servant!' he said. 'He *is* a servant!'

These words made Louise like and respect her husband less and less.

─────

One morning, Julien was walking in a small wood near the mayor's house and he met his two brothers. When they saw Julien's new suit of black clothes, they hated their younger brother more than ever. They beat him and left him lying on the ground. Louise de Rênal, who was also walking in the wood, found Julien.

When she saw that his face was covered in blood, Louise was shocked and horrified. She realized that the handsome young man could not return to his old life. And she began to understand that Julien was lonely and unhappy in his new life.

25

After this, Louise tried to talk to Julien more often. She asked him to walk with her in the garden. But as they walked alone together, Julien's education caused problems for him. He did not know how to behave in polite society. He did not know how to talk to Mme de Rênal. And he did not know what to say to her.

From that day, Julien was usually silent when he was alone with the mayor's wife. He became sullen and resentful[50]. When he *did* speak, he spoke foolishly. He *knew* that he said foolish things to Mme de Rênal. Often this made him hate her. And then he became even more resentful.

Did this make Louise de Rênal like Julien less? No, it did not. As the weeks passed, Louise began to like Julien more. She forgot that Julien did not know how to speak and behave correctly. She saw that he was intelligent and that he had strong opinions. But she also saw that he was sensitive. Julien showed his feelings when he was pleased or angry, happy or sad. And then something happened which made her think about her own feelings.

Louise de Rênal's maid was a young woman called Élisa. This young servant had fallen in love with Julien, but he did not know this. Then Élisa's aunt died and Élisa received the old woman's money. A few weeks later, Élisa asked Julien to marry her.

'We could live in a small house in the town,' Élisa told him. 'You could study law and become a lawyer. We could use my money while you learned about the law. We would be so happy.'

Of course, Louise heard this news.

'A marriage between Élisa and Julien will be good for both of them,' she thought. But she knew that she was not really happy about it. Was she a little jealous[51] of the maid?

'No, I'm not jealous,' Louise told herself. But she was not pleased about the news.

26

Julien was not pleased either. In fact, he refused to marry the maid. He was certainly not in love with her, but that was not his reason for refusing. He would not marry Élisa because he wanted to be rich and powerful. He wanted to live in a big city.

'And to do all this,' he told himself, 'I have to become a priest, not a lawyer in a small town. And I certainly don't want to be in love.'

Élisa was very unhappy. She told her problems to Curé Chélan, the old priest who had been teaching Julien about theology. The curé was a wise man. He knew about Julien's opinions and he understood Julien's feelings. When the young man told the curé that he could not marry Élisa because he wanted to be a priest, the old man was sad.

'I know what you want, Julien,' Curé Chélan said. 'But you want it for the wrong reasons. You don't love God. You don't really *believe* in God. You would be a very bad priest. But you could be a good lawyer. I want you to do what is right. You must think carefully about this.'

Julien listened to the old man. The curé loved him like a son and Julien was pleased. But the young man was not going to change his mind[52].

Curé Chélan told Élisa about Julien's decision and she was very unhappy. She wept for many days.

When Louise saw Élisa's tears, she asked the maid what was wrong and the girl told her.

Suddenly, Louise felt very happy. She realized that she *had* been jealous of the maid. And then Louise knew the truth. She had fallen in love with Julien Sorel herself.

Louise de Rênal had been only sixteen years old when she married the mayor. When she had married Rênal, she had not loved him. And she was not in love with him now. Louise had suddenly fallen in love with the nineteen-year-old tutor and her feelings were very strong.

'You don't really believe in God,' Curé Chelan said.

Louise was a proud woman, and sometimes she was afraid of her own feelings. If anyone found out about her love for Julien, she would bring trouble on her family. So Louise said nothing to anyone about her feelings.

And what were Julien's feelings for the mayor's wife? Well, he certainly did not love her. Sometimes Julien thought that he hated Mme de Rênal. But the truth was this: Julien did not hate Mme de Rênal herself. He was a poor peasant and she was rich. Her family was rich, and she had a lot of money of her own. The Rênals were members of the middle-class and it was this *class* that Julien hated. In fact, there were some days when Julien felt kindness towards the beautiful wife of his employer. He felt kindness because Mme de Rênal spoke well about him when her husband was cruel to him – and this happened often.

4

Vergy

When the spring arrived, there were great changes in Julien's life.

Every year, at the beginning of spring, the Rênals moved to their house in the country[53]. The mayor had this second house because he wanted to impress people. Each spring and summer, the aristocrats who stayed with the king left the royal palace outside Paris and stayed in their own houses in the country.

Rênal wanted to show his friends and neighbours that he was rich and important. So he had bought a house in the country too. His second house was in the village of Vergy, near the Jura Mountains.

The weather was sunny and warm when the Rênals arrived at Vergy. In the beautiful garden of M. de Rênal's house, brightly-coloured butterflies[54] flew from flower to flower. Julien bought a book about butterflies and quickly learned about them. Then he taught this knowledge to Louise and the children. Each afternoon, they all went into the garden and studied many different kinds of butterflies.

The mayor was not always in Vergy. Often, he had to stay in Verrières and look after his business. So this year, one of Louise's cousins – Mme Derville – came to Vergy to stay with the family for several weeks.

Julien liked Mme Derville. When he was with both women, he spoke more confidently. He felt less foolish. And he became less sullen and resentful. As Julien became more confident, he had longer conversations with Louise. And he soon began to realize that she was in love with him.

'One of these women must be my mistress[55]', he thought.

Julien did not love either of the women, but he wanted power. He often thought about his hero, Napoleon Bonaparte. When he was a young soldier, Napoleon had met a rich and beautiful woman called Josephine de Beauharnais. She had become Napoleon's mistress. In 1796 Napoleon had married Josephine and later they became Emperor and Empress of France.

'That is the way to succeed in the world,' Julien said to himself. 'I'll do the same thing as Napoleon. I must find a rich woman to be my mistress.'

'Madame Derville is intelligent and amusing,' Julien thought. 'I prefer[56] her, although she had not shown any interest[57] in *me*. But Mme de Rênal is already in love with me. And if I seduce[58] her, my position here will be less boring. And I'll have more power. Yes, I'll seduce the wife of the man who treats me like a servant. That is the way that I'll take my revenge[59] on Rênal.'

The evenings were now very warm. After the children had gone to bed, Julien, Mme Derville, and the mayor and his wife often sat in the garden together.

One lovely evening, Julien was sitting in the garden with the two women. The mayor was staying in Verrières that night.

While Mme Derville was talking, Julien touched one of Louise's hands and held it. It was very dark in the garden, so Mme Derville could not see what was happening.

At first, Louise pulled her hand away from Julien. But when Julien took her hand for the second time, Louise let her hand stay in his. Suddenly Julien felt very happy, and he gently pressed her hand with his fingers. When Louise pressed *his* hand, he smiled. Then he lifted her hand to his mouth and kissed her fingers.

That night, neither Louise or Julien could sleep. Louise thought about Julien's kisses and she was frightened. She knew that it was wrong to betray[60] her husband. But she was in love with Julien Sorel. She had never felt love like this before! Julien thought about Louise's husband. The mayor was an important and powerful man. If Julien seduced Rênal's beautiful wife, he would be in danger. He was sure that he would lose his job. Perhaps Rênal would kill him!

———

The next morning Julien was tired and he got up very late. When he went downstairs, he had a shock. Louise and Mme Derville were in the sitting-room with M. de Rênal. The mayor had arrived from Verrières early in the morning, and he was very angry.

'I pay you to teach my children, monsieur!' he said to Julien. 'But you haven't even spoken to them this morning. You're a bad tutor. I need to think about your future here. The children are in the garden now. Go and teach them! I'll speak to you later.'

Suddenly Julien felt very happy, and he gently pressed her hand with his fingers.

Half an hour later, Louise came into the garden to find Julien.

'Monsieur, I'm sorry that my husband was so rude to you,' she said.

'Madame,' Julien replied coldly. 'I am his servant. He is my employer. He can speak to me in any way that he wishes. He treats all his servants with contempt. But why is he here today?'

'He has brought new mattresses[61] for all the beds in the house,' Louise replied. 'He is with one of the servants. They are removing all the old mattresses from the bedrooms now.'

Suddenly, Julien's face became very pale.

'Madame, you must help me!' he said quickly. 'Under my mattress there's a small black box. Inside the box, there's a picture of ... of someone. Monsieur de Rênal mustn't see the picture. He's told me to stay in the garden, so I can't go to my room and get the box. Will you get it for me, madame? I'll be grateful for ever.'

Louise saw that Julien's body was shaking with fear.

'Yes, I'll do that for you,' she replied.

'And madame,' the young man continued. 'I must ask you to make a promise to me. Please don't look inside the box. Will you promise me that?'

Now Louise's face became pale too.

'I–I promise you,' she replied sadly. 'I won't look inside the box.'

Very strong feelings were in Louise's heart as she walked quickly towards the house. She loved Julien, and she hated the way that her husband had spoken to him. So she was happy to help Julien. But she was also very unhappy about the promise that he had asked for.

'Why mustn't I look in the box?' she said to herself. 'Whose portrait is in there? Is it a picture of another woman? Does Julien love someone else?'

As he watched Louise walk into the house, Julien was worried. There was not a portrait of a woman in the box under his mattress. There was a portrait of Napoleon Bonaparte.

'If anyone in the house finds out that I have a picture of Napoleon, I'll be sent away,' Julien thought. 'I hope that Madame de Rênal gets to my room before her husband.'

Ten minutes later, Louise found Julien in the garden again. She had the black box, and she had not opened it.

'Thank you, madame, you're very kind,' Julien said. 'There's something that I must do now. I'll see you this evening.'

Julien left Louise in the garden and he went into the house. A minute later he had thrown the box into the fire in the sitting-room. He had watched the box and the picture burn. Now he felt confident again. He was no longer afraid of his employer. But he was very, very angry with him.

'It's time to take my revenge on Rênal,' the young man said to himself. 'Rênal has power over me – that is true. But I understand his mind very well now. And I, too, have power.'

Julien went to find the mayor.

'Monsieur,' the young tutor said. 'You spoke rudely to me and the ladies heard this. That is wrong! Do you think that you can find a better tutor than me?'

He stopped speaking for a moment, but M. de Rênal did not reply.

'Ah, you *do* think that you can find a better teacher!' said Julien. 'Then you'll soon find out if you're right. Someone else wishes to employ me as a tutor. This person won't insult me. I'll go and work for him!'

The mayor immediately thought that one of his enemies wanted to employ Julien. Rênal knew that several people in Verrières were now richer than he was. Now, his enemies could pay for a tutor too.

'They're all Liberals and Jacobins!' Rênal thought angrily. 'I can't let anyone take this young man from my home.'

Ten minutes later, Rênal had promised to pay Julien more money. The young man would receive six hundred francs a year if he continued to teach the mayor's children. Rênal had also agreed that Julien could take three days' holiday. The holiday could start immediately. Now the young man knew whose power was greater.

That evening, Louise behaved coldly towards Julien. She did not look at him or speak to him. She was upset. She thought that Julien loved another woman. But Louise was proud, and she did not want Julien to see her unhappiness. She said nothing, so Julien behaved coldly too. And the next morning, he left the house very early. He did not tell Louise or Mme Derville where he was going. And he did not say goodbye to them.

When Louise heard that Julien had gone she was relieved[62], and she was terribly unhappy. She was relieved because now she could be faithful to her husband. But she was also very unhappy. She loved Julien and she wanted to be with him.

———

Julien had a friend – a timber merchant called Fouqué. Fouqué lived in a village on the other side of some high mountains.

Julien decided to visit Fouqué. He left Vergy and travelled north. For the first part of the day, Julien climbed the steep path that went up through the mountains.

When he reached the highest part of the path, he was very hot and tired. In the side of a steep mountain, he found a little cave.

'It's cool and quiet inside this cave,' the young man thought. 'I'll rest here for a while. No one else will come here.'

Julien sat in the cave and thought about everything that had happened that spring. Suddenly he wanted to write about it.

'I'm safe here,' he said to himself. 'I can write down my thoughts. In Rênal's house, it's dangerous to write down my ideas and feelings. But here, no one will ever find my words.'

Julien took some paper, a pen and some ink from his bag. For several hours, he wrote the history of his life as a tutor. Then he rested again.

Late in the afternoon, Julien made a fire and he burned all the paper that he had written on. Then he left the cave.

'I'll always remember this place,' he said to himself.

It was late in the evening when Julien reached Fouqué's house, but his friend was pleased to see him.

'So you've quarrelled with the mayor, Julien,' Fouqué said. 'Will you come to live here and work with me? I'll pay you well. I'll pay you much more than Rênal pays you. You'll have a good career as a timber merchant.'

Julien thought about his friend's offer. But he refused it.

'No, Fouqué. I've made a decision,' he said. 'I want to be a priest. I want to study at a seminary when I have saved some money.'

Fouqué was sad, but he accepted Julien's decision. And after this conversation, Julien enjoyed his holiday. But Fouqué spoke about women all the time, and this made Julien think about them too. The young timber merchant had had many mistresses, and he wanted to tell his friend about them.

As he walked back to Vergy on the third day, Julien thought about Louise de Rênal's love for him. He decided that it was time to use this love to succeed in the world.

A few days later, the mayor's wife became Julien's mistress.

'No, Fouqué. I've made a decision,' he said.
'I want to be a priest.'

5

Passion and Guilt[63]

For the first few days of their love affair, the relationship between Julien Sorel and Louise de Rênal was on different levels. Louise adored the beautiful young man, but he did not love her in the same way. Louise had betrayed her husband, and she felt guilty about this. But her adoration of Julien was much stronger than her feeling of guilt.

'My husband never loved me like this young man loves me,' Louise thought. 'But I'm much older than Julien. I wish that I had met him ten years ago.'

Of course, ten years before this Julien would have been nine years old! But Louise did not think about that. She could think of nothing and no one but the handsome young tutor. She was deeply in love. And most importantly, she believed that, at last, she was deeply loved.

In a strange way, Louise also enjoyed the young tutor's inexperience. Julien Sorel knew nothing about the world. He had been born in a small village and his family were simple peasants. Julien had never left Franche-Comté. In fact, he had never been to a city. He had never been told how to behave correctly. He was handsome, but he did not have good manners. And Julien had had no experience of love. He did not know how to behave with a woman. He did not know how to talk to someone who adored him. Most importantly, Julien did not know what to say to someone who was his equal[64] when they were alone together. Louise realized that she could teach the sensitive young scholar about the world. And this made her very happy.

However, Louise did *not* know that whatever Julien said to her, he did not love her. Sometimes, when they were alone together, Julien wept like a girl because his mistress was so beautiful. But he had not wanted Louise to be his mistress because of her beauty. He had wanted her to be his mistress because of the power that it gave him. During those first days of their affair, Julien behaved like an actor. He thought about everything that he said and did when he was with Louise.

Each morning, before daylight, Louise quietly left Julien's bed and returned to her own bedroom. When she had left, Julien thought about their night together.

'Did I do the right things?' he asked himself. 'And did I say the right things?'

Julien did not know how lovers should talk to each other. So he recited words that characters from books say to each other. When he said these things to Louise, they were often the 'wrong things'!

Louise behaved in exactly the right way towards Julien. She pretended that she did not to see or hear the young man's mistakes. When her lover behaved incorrectly, Louise pretended not to notice his bad manners. She was sweet and kind, but she was not a clever woman. And because her own education had been simple, she admired Julien's intelligence.

'He's clever and he's a good scholar,' Louise thought. 'He is – or will be – good at anything.'

When Julien saw that Louise admired him, he stopped worrying. He no longer behaved like an actor. And soon, Julien realized that he really *was* in love with Louise de Rênal.

———

For several months, life at Vergy was happy for Julien and Louise. The mayor was often away in Verrières. The lovers were alone together more and more often. Soon Louise's cousin realized what had happened. Madame Derville noticed that Louise had bought new, pretty clothes. Mme

Derville saw the looks of love between Julien and Louise and she tried to warn[65] her cousin.

'Louise, please don't become too fond of the young tutor,' Mme Derville said. 'He's only a servant, a peasant. Don't do anything which will make your husband angry.'

But Louise did not want to listen to her cousin's warning. So a few days later, Mme Derville decided to leave Vergy.

After Mme Derville left, the lovers were alone together for much of the time. Julien and Louise were passionately in love with each other. When they were together, they forgot about everything else.

Sometimes, Louise tried to understand why this clever young man loved her so much.

'Perhaps he'll soon stop loving me,' she told herself. 'Perhaps he'll fall in love with a younger woman.'

But Julien never showed her that he wanted anyone else. And soon Louise stopped worrying.

———

In the early summer, the Rênal family had to return to Verrières for a week. The little town was going to have important visitors. The king of a foreign country was coming to Franche-Comté and he was going to visit the town of Verrières. In a tomb in the old church at Verrières, the body of a famous saint was buried.

The King of —— wanted to say prayers by the tomb of this holy man. Because Rênal was the town's mayor, the foreign king was going to stay at Rênal's house. For many hours, the servants cleaned the house and prepared it for the royal visitor.

'The king is going to be accompanied[66] by two important people,' said Rênal. 'One of these companions is an aristocrat – the Marquis de La Mole. For more than two hundred years, the marquis's ancestors[67] have been the governors of Franche-Comté. The king's other companion will be the Bishop of

Agde. He is Monsieur de La Mole's nephew. The bishop will lead a special ceremony in the church.'

All the important people of Verrières were going to greet the King of ——. A guard of honour[68] was going to stand beside the road as the king, the bishop and the aristocrat went past in a carriage.

The mayor decided that Julian should be a member of the guard of honour. For this ceremony, the mayor's tailor made Julien a special suit of clothes. The young man was going to wear a new blue and silver coat, instead of his black clothes. The mayor had also borrowed[69] a horse which Julien was going to ride.

The morning of the visit arrived. Julien sat on the horse and waited for the carriage. He did not know how to ride a horse, but he was lucky. He did not fall off it! The sun shone on Julien's blue and silver coat. And it shone on the bright metal of Julien's spurs and sword[70]. The big brown horse danced in the road and everyone admired the handsome young tutor. Julien was delighted. He was an important person on an important day!

Julien was impressed by both the marquis and the bishop. But he was impressed in different ways. The Marquis de La Mole was a small man who wore plain clothes. But around his neck, he wore a pale blue ribbon which had a medal on it. Julien found out that the Church had given this honour to the marquis. And it was an honour given to very few people. The Marquis de La Mole was a very powerful man. His friends had important positions in the government. Julien thought that the marquis looked arrogant[71] as well as powerful.

After the carriage passed him, Julien rode quickly to the church on a different road. He was going to meet Curé Chélan. When he reached the church, Julien removed his new blue coat and put on his black coat again.

41

The big brown horse danced in the road and everyone admired the handsome young tutor.

Curé Chélan introduced Julien to the Bishop of Agde, who was kind and pleasant to the young tutor. Then the bishop went into a room at the side of the church.

Julien had been surprised when he saw the Bishop of Agde. The bishop was a young man.

'He is only ten years older than me!' Julien said to himself. 'I thought that all bishops were old men with grey hair. The Marquis de La Mole must have used all his power to get his nephew this very important position. I was right. The Church has the most power in this country now. I can never be an aristocrat. But if I become a priest, I will get power too.'

When everything inside the church was ready, the curé spoke to Julien.

'Go to Monseigneur the Bishop[72]. Tell him that we are ready for him,' the curé told his young friend. 'The ceremony can begin now.'

Julien walked into the room very quietly. It was a very large room, and the bishop did not hear Julien enter. For a minute, Julien stood and looked in amazement.

At the other end of the room, the Bishop of Agde was standing in front of a large mirror. He was looking at his beautiful robes. Suddenly the bishop lifted his hand, moved it from side to side, then let it fall. Then he did the same thing again – and again, and again.

'He's practising!' Julien told himself. 'He's like an actor practising his part in a play. The bishop is practising how to give a blessing[73] to the people! He reminds me of me!'

At that moment, Julien understood a lot of things about the young bishop and the marquis. And at the same time, he understood about the power of the Church and the power of the aristocrats in France.

———

Soon after the Rênal family returned to Vergy, life changed for Julien and Louise. The mayor's youngest son, Stanislas, suddenly became very ill. Louise blamed[74] herself for this. Her guilt was terrible. She was a religious woman. She believed in God and the laws written in the Bible.

'This terrible thing has happened because of me, Julien,' the unhappy woman told her lover. 'I've broken one of God's laws. The Bible says that adultery[75] is wrong – it's a sin. I've loved you and betrayed my husband. That is why Stanislas is ill. God is punishing me because of my sins. He's punishing me for loving you. God is punishing me because I have betrayed my husband. What shall we do?'

For several days, everybody believed that Stanislas was going to die. His mother became more and more upset. Her feeling of guilt became stronger and stronger.

'I can't go on living like this,' Louise told Julien one night. 'I must tell my husband the truth about us. I must tell him that we are lovers. Then he'll punish me and perhaps God will let my son live. My husband will send me away. I'll never see my sons again. But that doesn't matter. I only want Stanislas to get well.'

'No, don't tell your husband!' Julien replied. 'If M. de Rênal sends you away, everyone in Verrières and Vergy will know that he has an unfaithful[76] wife. Everyone will laugh at him and tell jokes about him. If he finds out the truth, it will kill him, madame!'

Julien was not really very worried about Rênal. But he was worried about what would happen to *him*, if the mayor found out about his affair with Louise.

'You're right! I won't tell my husband about us,' Louise replied. 'But you must go away, Julien. I must send you away, my dear love. I can't be with you any more.'

Julien *did* leave Vergy, but two days later he came back. Louise had sent him a message. It said that she could not go on living without him. She told him that he must return.

After Julien returned, Louise knew that she loved the

44

young man more than anyone or anything. She loved him more than she loved God's laws, her husband, and her son.

Julien behaved well at this time. He now loved Louise very much. Every night, he held her in his arms while she wept. He did not ask her to make any promises to him. Of course, he still made speeches which he had read in books.

'Shall I go and live in a monastery[77], madame?' he asked his lover one night. 'Shall I join a group of priests who are never allowed to speak? Will God forgive us then?'

Julien's words came from books, but he spoke sincerely. He truly meant what he said.

Then suddenly, Stanislas began to get better. In a few days, the little boy was well again. And after this, Louise believed that the end of her love for Julien was God's punishment. She knew that they could not be together for ever.

'No one has ever felt such passion and joy, as well as such sadness and guilt!' she told herself. 'I know that our affair must end – that is my punishment.'

So the lovers' lives continued until one day in early September. And on that day, Rênal received a letter which was written on blue paper.

6

Letters on Blue Paper

What had happened was this: Rênal's servant, Élisa, had been talking to Monsieur Valenod.

The town of Verrières was controlled by only a few men, and they were all rich. These merchants pretended to like each other, but they did not. Each merchant wanted all the money and power for himself. Each merchant thought that the other businessmen in the town were his enemies.

The richest and most powerful man in Verrières was the mayor, M. de Rênal, and his chief enemy was M. Valenod. Rênal had become mayor because he had the greatest number of powerful friends. Rênal and Valenod pretended to be friends. But the truth was this: They hated each other.

Valenod was jealous because Rênal had a tutor for his children. But Valenod also had another, more special reason to be jealous of the mayor. For a long time, Valenod had been secretly in love with Rênal's wife.

Louise de Rênal disliked Valenod. She thought that he was one of the rude, bad-mannered people who made life in Verrières unpleasant. Valenod was not clever and he did not understand that Louise would never like him. Every few weeks, he wrote her a letter. Valenod always wrote his letters on blue paper. The letters said foolish and untruthful things. Whenever one of these letters arrived, Louise put it in a desk in her room and she forgot about it. She never told her husband about these letters.

The mayor was not the only person with enemies. Julien had enemies too. Several people who worked in the mayor's house were jealous of the young tutor. And the person who hated him most was Élisa. Julien had refused to marry the maid and she wanted revenge.

Maids usually know many things about their employers. And by this time, Élisa knew all about Louise's secret and passionate affair with Julien. She also knew that Valenod loved Louise. So one day, when Élisa met Valenod in Verrières, she told him what was happening in Vergy when the mayor was away. Élisa knew what Valenod would do next.

When he heard about the secret affair between Louise de Rênal and the young tutor, Valenod was angry and even more jealous. Then he thought of a way to hurt his enemy and his enemy's wife. He wrote a letter to Rênal and told him how his wife had betrayed him. Valenod did not sign his name at the end of the letter. He sent it anonymously.

———

The anonymous letter arrived at Vergy one Friday evening. The mayor and Julien were sitting together when a servant brought the letter into the dining-room. Julien watched Rênal's face become pale as he read the words on the blue paper. Every few seconds, the mayor stopped reading and looked at Julien. These looks were not friendly, but he did not say anything. Julien began to guess what had happened.

'Someone has written to M. de Rênal and told him about my affair with Louise,' Julien thought. 'But he doesn't know if the words in the letter are true or false. And the letter must be anonymous because he hasn't asked *me* about it.'

Later that evening, Julien found Louise in the garden.

'Madame, please don't come to my room tonight,' he whispered to her. 'I think that someone has written an anonymous letter to your husband. It was written on blue paper. M. de Rênal doesn't know who wrote the letter. And he doesn't know if the news is true or false. We must be very careful. Your husband mustn't see us together.'

———

Very early the next morning, a servant brought a book to Julien's room.

'Page one hundred and thirty, monsieur,' the servant said quickly and quietly, and then he went away.

Julien opened the book at page one hundred and thirty. He found two pieces of paper there. On one of the pieces of paper there was a message from Louise. The second piece of paper was blue and there was nothing written on it.

Julien read Louise's message.

47

My *love*

This is what we must do. First, you must write an anonymous letter to me. To make the letter, cut words from the pages of this book. Then glue[78] the words onto the blue paper. In the letter, you must threaten[79] to tell my husband that you and I are lovers. Say that I must become your mistress, or you'll tell everyone the truth. Don't sign the letter.

I'll show my husband the letter. He'll suspect that it comes from Valenod – I'll make sure that he thinks this. Then I'll pretend that everything in the letter is untrue. I'll tell my husband to send you away. He'll send you to the house in Verrières while he finds out what is happening.

When you get to Verrières, you must meet Valenod and the other rich merchants who hate my husband. Make sure that everyone in Verrières knows about these meetings. Valenod and his friends have always been jealous of my husband. When they heard that he'd employed you, they wanted a tutor for their own children. My husband will think that one of his enemies wants you to be dismissed[80]. He'll believe that one of these rich merchants wants to employ you.

My husband will believe that Valenod – his worst enemy – is trying to trick him. He'll remember the first letter that he received and he'll believe that Valenod wrote it. Of course, this is true. After Élisa told him about our affair, Valenod did write the first letter. But now my husband will think that both letters are part of Valenod's trick – a trick to get you dismissed. Then he won't believe the words in the first letter.

If I don't see you tomorrow, goodbye my love, but not for long.

Julien did what Louise wanted him to do. He cut words from the book and glued them onto the piece of blue paper.

Later that day, Louise was walking in the garden. Suddenly, she saw her husband coming towards her. Rênal looked extremely angry.

'He's going to speak to me about the anonymous letter,' Louise said to herself. 'I must speak first. I must be a very good actor now. He must believe everything that I say and do.'

'My dear husband, I'm glad to meet you here!' she said angrily. 'Read this letter. Someone has insulted my honour[81]!'

Louise gave her husband the piece of blue paper with the words glued onto it. He read these words:

Madame
You must do what I say. I know your secret. Unless you become my mistress, I'll tell your husband about your betrayal. I'll tell him about your love affair with the tutor. Remember, madame, you are in my power, for ever.

Rênal finished reading the letter and looked at his wife. He saw tears in her eyes.

'Everything in that letter is a terrible lie!' Louise said. She pretended to be angry and upset. 'And I hope that you don't believe any of it. But you must send the tutor away. Give the little peasant some money and send him back to his family. I can't allow people to believe these lies! Julien Sorel mustn't stay in our house for a day longer.'

'Of course I don't believe this letter, madame,' Rênal replied. 'But who wrote it? The writer hasn't signed his name and I never believe anonymous letters. But we must find out who *did* write it.'

Then suddenly, he said, 'Have you had any other letters that I don't know about? Please tell me.'

'They ... they were not like this one, monsieur,' Louise replied. 'They were not anonymous letters.'

'But you *have* received other letters which I don't know about?' her husband asked, suspiciously[82].

Louise said nothing.

49

'Answer me, madame!' her husband shouted.

'Well, M. Valenod writes to me sometimes,' she replied. 'They're foolish and untruthful letters, so I don't tell you about them.'

'Where are these letters?' said the mayor. 'You must show me! Now!'

'Monsieur, they're private letters to me,' Louise replied. 'They're locked in a desk in my room. I shall certainly not give you the key.'

'Stay here!' shouted the mayor. 'I don't need a key!'

As she watched her husband walking quickly towards the house, Louise smiled.

An hour later, Louise went her room. She saw that the locks of her desk had been broken. Valenod's letters, which had been written on blue paper, had been taken from the desk. The letters had been torn into pieces and thrown onto the floor. Suddenly, Louise felt happy and confident. But when she met her husband, she pretended to be angry again.

'When are you sending that peasant boy away?' she asked Rênal. 'He can't stay here. Valenod has told lies about the tutor and me. I can't have my honour insulted.'

'To please you, I'll send Julien to Verrières,' the mayor replied. 'He'll stay there for two weeks, but he'll stay in my house. I'll not send him back to his father's house. Julien has done nothing wrong. I'll not let him go and work for someone else. And I'll certainly not let him go to Valenod! Valenod has been a guest in our house! He has he dined with us! But now I find out that he writes love letters to you! And he writes anonymous letters to me because he wants to steal my tutor. He will not succeed!'

That evening, the lovers met secretly.

'My plan worked,' Louise whispered. 'My husband will send you to Verrières tomorrow. We're safe. I love you, Julien.'

'Well, M. Valenod writes to me sometimes. They're foolish and untruthful letters, so I don't tell you about them.'

7

Julien's Choice

As soon as Julien arrived at the house in Verrières, he began to receive invitations. They were invitations from rich men who wanted Julien to work for them. Suddenly, all these men needed tutors for their children – especially Valenod! Soon, Valenod had offered Julien eight hundred francs a year if he would be tutor to his family. Julien did not want to work for the mayor's enemy, but he did not give Valenod an answer immediately.

A few days later, Valenod invited Julien to dine with his family. And at Valenod's house, Julien met several other powerful men from the area.

'I dislike all these dishonest and corrupt men,' the young tutor thought. 'They're worse than Rênal!' But he was polite to them.

———

Louise de Rênal's plan had worked and she was safe. Her husband wanted to believe that she was innocent. This was because Rênal wanted Louise's money. She knew why her husband behaved in this way. In a few years, Louise was going to receive a lot of money from her relatives. If Rênal sent her away, he would never get Louise's money. So when he received more anonymous letters, Rênal decided to forget about them.

Louise continued to pretend that she was a faithful wife. She was a good actor. She often spoke about the insults to her honour. But whenever she asked her husband to send Julien away, he would not do this. And she knew that he would always refuse. Rênal could not allow Julien to work for anyone else. Whenever Louise spoke about dismissing Julien,

Rênal thought about his enemy, Valenod. The mayor refused to talk to his wife about Julien.

———

At the end of the autumn, the mayor's family left the house in Vergy and returned to live in Verrières. Julien still visited Louise's room every night. He loved her deeply, and now he loved her children very much too. She knew this, and it made her very happy. Perhaps she also knew that people were talking about her affair with the young tutor. But she did not care. Her husband refused to believe the story of her adultery, so Louise continued her affair with Julien.

'If Valenod sends me one more letter about you, I'll fight him and kill him!' Rênal told her one day.

Louise wept and told her husband not to fight Valenod.

'If Rênal fights Valenod,' she thought, 'Valenod will probably kill him. Of course, I don't want my husband to die. But if he died, I'd be a rich widow. And then I could marry Julien. We would have to leave Franche-Comté. But we would be happy for ever.'

———

It was Élisa who destroyed[83] Louise's happiness. The maid was still angry with Julien and with Mme de Rênal. Élisa had told Valenod that Louise was having an affair with the tutor. But the maid's plan for revenge had failed. She now thought of another plan. She decided to betray Julien.

One day, Élisa went to the church to speak to Curé Chélan. She pretended that she was very worried. And she pretended that she wanted God's help with a problem. She asked the priest to give her advice. When the curé asked Élisa what she was worried about, she told him about Mme de Rênal's affair with Julien.

Curé Chélan loved Julien like a son. But the curé believed in God, and he believed that people should obey God's laws. Julien had broken God's law about adultery. This law said it

She told him about Mme de Rênal's affair with Julien.

was a sin for someone to have an affair with another person's husband or wife. Anyone who broke God's laws was a sinner. Sinners could not go to heaven after they died. The curé wanted to remind Julien about God's law. He decided to give him some advice and a warning. So he sent a message to the mayor's house. The old priest asked Julien to visit him.

'Julien, please don't lie to me,' the curé said, quietly and seriously. 'I know that you'll try to protect a woman's honour. I won't ask you any questions. I'll just give you two choices. But first, I must tell you this: You have to leave Verrières. When you have left the town, you must choose what to do next. Either you must go to live with your friend Fouqué and be a timber merchant. Or, if you still want to be a priest, you must go to the seminary in Besançon. You can start your training there.

'If you do want to be a priest,' the old man continued, 'you must go to the seminary immediately. My dear Julien, we have talked about your career before. You want to be a priest. But I don't believe that you want to be a priest for the right reasons. If you still want this career, I'll write to the Abbé Pirard about you. He's the director of the seminary in Besançon and he's an old friend of mine. I've known Abbé Pirard for thirty years, and he's a good man.'

Julien loved Louise and he loved her children. He was happy in Verrières. He knew that Rênal could not harm him because the mayor wanted his wife's money. But Julien believed that priests had all the power in France. In fact, since his meeting with the Bishop of Agde, Julien believed this more strongly than ever. He decided to go to Besançon and become a priest.

That night, he told Louise that he must leave Verrières.

'We shall meet again,' he said sadly. Then he kissed her gently. 'And I shall always love you.'

8

The Seminary

Besançon was the main town of Franche-Comté. Julien had never visited the town, so he walked through the streets for several hours, looking at everything. It was late in the evening when he reached the seminary.

Half an hour after the seminary's heavy wooden door had closed behind him, Julien was standing in front of a terrifying man. The man was sitting at a desk and he was wearing the black clothes of a priest. The terrifying priest had not looked up once since Julien had gone into his room. He had been writing.

Suddenly, the priest looked up at Julien. The skin on the priest's nose, cheeks and chin was very red. But the skin on his forehead was very pale. His hair was black and his eyes were small and bright. Immediately, Julien knew that this man could guess his thoughts and feelings.

'Who are you?' the black-haired priest asked. His voice did not sound kind.

'My name is Julien Sorel,' the frightened young man replied.

'Ah,' said the priest. 'Well, you're very late, monsieur! You should have arrived earlier.'

Then he opened a drawer in his desk and took out a letter.

'I've received a letter about you from my old friend, Curé Chélan, in Verrières,' the priest went on. He started to read the latter aloud.

My dear friend

I'm sending to you a young man whose name is Julien Sorel. He's twenty years old and I've known him all his life. Julien wants to become a priest. But he'll need a scholarship – he cannot

56

'Who are you?' the black-haired priest asked.

pay for his training. His father has money, but he gives Julien nothing. The young man is intelligent and he learns easily. His memory is good. He knows Latin, and I've also taught him some theology. But are his reasons for wanting to be a priest the right ones? I don't know. If you think that Julien will be a good priest, please let him join the seminary. I hope that you'll be able to give him a scholarship. If you don't think that Julien should be a priest, then send him back to me. He'll become a timber merchant.

The director put the letter down on his desk.

'There are three hundred and twenty young men studying in this seminary,' he said. His voice was now softer and kinder. 'They all want to be priests. But only eight of them have been sent to me by good men. Monsieur Sorel, my old friend Curé Chélan is a good man. He has asked me to help you and I will do this. But you must work hard. You must work harder than all the young men whose fathers are paying for their training. If I see that you *are* working hard, then I'll be pleased with you.'

'Monsieur, you must be Abbé Pirard,' Julien said. 'My friend, Curé Chélan, told me that you were a fine man. Thank you for talking to me.'

Suddenly, Abbé Pirard started speaking to Julien in Latin. He asked the young man many questions about the Bible and found that Julien knew the Bible well. But when they started to talk about theology, the abbé soon realized that Julien did not have any opinions of his own. The young man simply repeated the opinions that he had read in books. Often, these opinions contradicted each other[84]. But Julien did not seem to understand this. He believed that if writers' thoughts were printed in books, all their opinions must be true. Abbé Pirard was amused, but he did not let the young man see this.

It was three hours before Abbé Pirard finished asking questions. Then, for the first time, he smiled at Julien. He picked up a small bell that was on his desk and rang it. A few minutes later, an old servant came into the room.

'Take Monsieur Sorel to cell[85] one hundred and three,' the director said to the servant. 'He is now a member of this seminary.'

————

Julien was soon bored with his studies at the seminary. He was not interested in any of the other students, so he did not become their friend.

Most of the students were the sons of peasants, like him. But *unlike* Julien, most of the students were stupid. Julien and the other students were not really interested in theology. They all wanted to be priests for the wrong reasons – they were only interested in power and money. In country areas of France, priests earned a lot of money.

The stupid and greedy students hated Julien because they did not understand him. They hated the young man because his memory was better than theirs and he knew more Latin. When Julien got the highest marks in theology classes, they attacked him. And they tried to make trouble for him with the teachers.

Although most of the students were stupid and greedy, there were some students who were very pious. They had a strong belief in God. They studied the Bible and they behaved well.

But these students hated Julien because they *understood* him. The pious students knew that Julien only *pretended* to believe in God and the Bible. And they knew that he was not really interested in theology.

One day, Julien was walking next to a pious student in the garden of the seminary. Suddenly there was the sound of loud thunder. Bright flashes of lightning lit up the sky and rain began to fall. The two young men were in the middle of a storm. The pious student pushed Julien away from him.

'Don't stand next to me!' the student shouted. 'God knows that you don't believe in him. He's trying to kill you with his lightning! You should die. But he mustn't kill me too!'

———

The days and months at the seminary passed slowly for Julien. He was bored and unhappy.

Abbé Pirard liked Julien, but he could not help him. At the time that Julien was studying in the seminary, the most powerful men of the French church were Jesuits[86]. Jesuits believed that only the Pope in Rome could tell the members of the Church in France what to do. And the Jesuits believed that only the Pope could tell people what to believe. The Jesuits controlled many of the seminaries in France, and they controlled the seminary in Besançon. And some of these powerful men were suspicious of Abbé Pirard himself. They thought that he secretly believed in the ideas of the Jansenists[87]. So the abbé had to be very careful. If the other teachers saw Abbé Pirard helping Julien, the abbé would have trouble.

There was one person in Besançon who believed that Julien was honest and truthful. He also believed that Julien would be a good priest. This person was Abbé Chas-Bernard. Abbé Chas-Bernard prepared all the religious ceremonies in the great cathedral[88] of Besançon. The abbé was also a teacher at the seminary. He loved beautiful things and he especially liked to make the cathedral look beautiful. He saw that Julien was the best student in his class. The abbé believed that Julien liked the holy places to be beautiful too.

Abbé Chas-Bernard asked Julien to help him. The abbé had to prepare the cathedral for the festival[89] of Corpus Christi. This was one of the most important religious festivals of the year. First, there was going to be a ceremony in the cathedral. Then, the Bishop of Besançon was going to lead a great procession[90] out of the huge building and around the town. While the bishop lead the procession around Besançon, priests would ring the great bells of the cathedral. Finally, the procession would return to the cathedral.

For Corpus Christi, the inside of the cathedral had to look beautiful. Thousands of candles would be lit, and many special decorations would put inside the building.

Abbé Chas-Bernard had bought hundreds of metres of expensive red silk and many beautiful long birds' feathers from Paris. He wanted Julien to fasten long pieces of the red material to the great stone pillars which held up the roof of the cathedral. These pillars were more than ten metres high. The abbé also wanted Julien to fasten the feathers near the ceiling, high inside the cathedral.

None of the other students wanted to help the abbé. They did not want to go up the tall ladders[91] to the high ceiling. They were too frightened. But Julien was not frightened. When he was a boy, he had often climbed high up onto the machinery in his father's sawmill. So, as soon as he arrived in the cathedral, Julien began to run up and down the wooden ladders. He quickly fastened the pieces of silk to the pillars and he fastened the long feathers near the ceiling.

When Julien's work was finished, the cathedral looked wonderful. Abbé Chas-Bernard was very pleased with his helper.

'I'm very grateful to you, my young friend,' he said to Julien. 'I'll tell the bishop and Abbé Pirard about all the help that you have given me.'

By the time that the Corpus Christi ceremony started, Julien's thoughts had changed. When he heard the great cathedral bells ringing, Julien stopped thinking about the cost of the expensive decorations. And for a while, he stopped hating the Church. The priest that Julien had helped that day loved beauty. And Julien began to love beauty too.

He quickly fastened the pieces of silk to the pillars.

9
—

Changes

A few days later, Abbé Pirard came to Julien's cell and spoke to him.

'I've received a letter from Abbé Chas-Bernard,' he told him. 'He says good things about you, Julien. And I'm pleased with your work here too. You have a good mind. And I think you that have a good heart.

'I've worked here for fifteen years,' the director went on. 'But in a few weeks' time, I'll have to leave this seminary. My enemies are making me leave. I'm going to resign[92] from my position. But before I leave, I want to do something for you. From today, you'll be a tutor here as well as a student. You'll help the other students to study the Bible.'

Julien was happy and very surprised. Tears fell from his eyes, and he kissed the abbé's hand.

'I like you, Julien. I wish you well in your future life,' the director said after a few moments. 'I wish you well, but I'm worried about you too. Stupid people will always dislike you. Jealous people will try to destroy you. Your life will not be easy. You must have courage. You must pray to God. He will help you. You must always love the truth more than you love any person.'

———

After this conversation, Abbé Pirard was very careful. He made sure that he was never alone with Julien. Many of the other students were jealous of Julien and the director did not want them to punish the young man. But in fact, life at the seminary was easier for Julien in the weeks after he became a tutor. He now taught many of the students, who began to respect him.

Although most of the students respected him now, some of Abbé Pirard's enemies started to hate Julien. This was because the director had made Julien a tutor.

At the end of the year there were examinations. It was at this time that Abbé Pirard's enemies took their revenge on Julien. Several of Abbé Pirard's enemies were examiners for the seminary. They had to test all the students' knowledge. There were two hundred and thirty students in the class. Julien was placed second. When they saw that Julien had done very well in the first few examinations, the examiners became angry.

For the last examination, Julien was asked questions about the Bible. An elderly priest asked Julien if he knew the poems of the Roman poet, Horace. These were not religious poems, they were poems about love. They were written in Latin. Many years ago, Julien had read the poetry of Horace. And because he had a wonderful memory, he now began to talk about the poems. He remembered every word of them and he began to recite them. He made no mistakes. He thought that he was impressing the examiner, but he was wrong.

'Stop, monsieur!' the elderly priest said suddenly. 'You haven't used your time in this seminary well! You're here to study theology. You're not here to study love poems!'

When the final examination results were announced, Julien was placed at number one hundred and ninety-eight. Abbé Pirard was very angry, but he could not help Julien. For the next few days, he watched Julien carefully. But the young man did not seem to be angry about what had happened. In fact, he did not seem to care.

———

A few days later, Abbé Pirard sent Julien to the house of the Bishop of Besançon with a letter. It was the director's letter of resignation from the seminary. The bishop read the letter quickly, then he began to talk to Julien. They talked about the Bible and they talked about Latin poetry. The bishop enjoyed his conversation with Julien very much.

Then the bishop started to talk about Horace. He loved the Roman poet's work. Julien and the bishop were soon reciting lines of Horace's poetry.

Before Julien returned to the seminary, the bishop gave him a gift – some beautiful books of Latin poetry.

Abbé Pirard did not have many friends in Besançon, but he had a good friend in Paris. And this friend was a rich and powerful aristocrat – the Marquis de La Mole. When the marquis heard that Abbé Pirard's enemies had made the abbé leave the seminary in Besançon, he decided to help. He found a new job for the abbé. Abbé Pirard was going to work in one of the most important churches in Paris.

A few days later, the two men were talking together.

'I'm too busy,' Marquis de La Mole told his friend. 'I have too much work to do. I need someone to help me with my papers. I need a secretary.'

'Ah, I know someone who would do that job well,' Pirard replied. 'He's a young man who is studying at the seminary in Besançon. His name is Julien Sorel. At the moment, Julien only knows about theology. But he learns quickly. He could learn to be your secretary. And he could be very useful to you.'

A few days after this conversation, Julien received a letter. The letter gave him instructions to travel to Paris and it contained some money. So after fourteen months, Julien left the seminary in Besançon. But he did not start his journey to Paris immediately. First he went to visit Fouqué, to tell his friend about his new position.

'Julien, this job will be dangerous,' the timber merchant said. 'You're a good Liberal, but the Marquis de la Mole is an Ultra. All the time that you work for him, you'll have to be dishonest. Stay here with me and become an honest timber merchant. It will be a better career for you. I'm afraid that you'll be destroyed if you go to Paris.'

'I worked for more than a year for Rênal, who was an Ultra, and I wasn't destroyed,' Julien thought. 'I was in the seminary for fourteen months, pretending to believe in God. And that didn't destroy me. I'm good at being dishonest!'

And now he wanted to be with powerful men who made decisions about the government of France. So Julien did not listen to Fouqué's advice. But when he left Besançon the next day, he travelled to Verrières, not Paris.

'I must see her again!' he said to himself.

———

It was late at night when Julien arrived at Rênal's house in Verrières. He walked quietly towards the wall that surrounded the garden. He was carrying a wooden ladder which he had bought from a peasant. He put the ladder against the wall and climbed it. A few minutes later, Julien was walking through the garden, carrying the ladder. At last, he was standing below the window of Louise's room.

Julien looked up at the place where he had stayed for so many nights. There was no light shining from the room.

'Perhaps she's already asleep,' Julien thought.

He threw some small stones up at the window, but his mistress did not look out. So he placed the ladder against the wall of the house. Then he climbed the ladder and knocked on the window with his fingers.

'Madame, it's me – Julien,' he called quietly. 'Please open the window.'

A moment later, Louise de Rênal was looking out through the glass. When she saw him, she was horrified.

'Why have you come here?' she asked angrily. 'You must leave immediately. If you don't go, I'll call my husband!'

'Please don't send me away,' Julien said. 'I love you so

much. I've thought about you every day and every night. Do you no longer love me?'

'Ah, Julien, didn't you get my letter?' Louise asked, more gently.

'I've had no letter, madame,' Julien replied. 'For fourteen months, I've had no messages from you. I've been miserable. What has happened here?'

'I wrote to you at the seminary,' Louise replied. 'I said that I could never see you again. I said that I could never hate you. But our love made me guilty of many sins, and I hated that. Julien, I was so unhappy after you left. And my cousin, Mme Derville, told me every day that I was a sinner. She told me that my sins were making me unhappy. So I told Curé Chélan what had happened, and I asked him to help me. The curé was very kind to me. But he told me that I should only think of my husband. He told me to write to you and say goodbye forever. He told me to forget you. And I promised him that I would forget you.'

Julien thought for a minute. Then he said sadly, 'Abbé Pirard must have kept your letter,' he said. 'He didn't tell me about it. He wanted me to forget you too. He knew that if I read your letter, I would come to you.'

'I'm sorry, Julien, but you must leave now.'

'Please let me in. I want to hear about your life since I left your house.'

'Julien is talking too loudly,' Louise thought. 'If a servant hears us and finds us together, there will be trouble for both of us.'

She opened the window.

'You can come in for a few minutes,' she said. 'But then you must leave. You must leave and never come back. Please promise me this.'

Julien climbed into the room, then he pulled the ladder up behind him.

'What are you doing?' Louise asked, horrified and afraid.

'If I leave the ladder against the wall,' Julien replied, 'a servant might see it.'

Julien and Louise sat on the bed and talked. They talked about their sadness since they had parted a year before. Tears ran down Julien's cheeks. Louise was always upset when Julien cried. Half an hour later, she was lying in his arms. And she had forgotten the promises she had asked Julien to make.

———

Daylight was coming into the bedroom. It was dawn.

'Julien, you must leave,' Louise said quietly. 'Soon the servants will be starting their work in the house. They mustn't see you here.'

'Madame, I have to go to Paris,' Julien replied. 'Perhaps we'll never meet again. Please let me stay here today. Hide me in your room and let us be together for one more night. I'll leave before dawn tomorrow.'

Louise knew that she should send Julien away. For a year, she had tried to love her husband. But he had been cold and suspicious. Now she remembered how this young man had loved her.

'Very well,' she said. 'But Élisa will come to this room soon. Madame Derville is not staying in the house at the moment. You must hide in her room during the day. I'll bring food to you there. And we must hide the ladder before Élisa comes.'

Louise carefully opened the door, then she took the ladder and put it outside her room.

'I'll ask a servant to move it later,' she said.

———

Julien hid in Mme Derville's room. He saw Louise for only a few minutes during the day. But in the evening she came to him, took him into her room, and locked the door.

68

'I told the servants that I felt ill,' she said. 'I told them that I had a headache and needed to rest. I've brought some food for us. But I'm a little worried. Someone has moved the ladder. I don't know who took it away. But my husband hasn't said anything about it.'

They had been talking quietly for half an hour when someone knocked loudly on the door. They heard Rênal's voice outside.

'Let me in, madame!' he called.

Julien quickly hid under the bed and Louise unlocked the door. The mayor entered the room noisily.

'Why are you eating alone in here, with the door locked?' Rênal asked suspiciously.

'I had a headache, I needed to rest,' his wife replied. As she spoke, she removed her dress and quickly threw it over a chair on which Julien had left his hat. Rênal had not seen the hat lying there.

'I'm tired and I need to sleep,' Louise said.

'Well, if you want to sleep, I'll leave you now,' Rênal said. 'Perhaps you'll feel better soon.'

He left the room and Louise locked the door behind him.

An hour later, she and Julien were lying in each other's arms. They had been apart for a year, but now they were happy. Suddenly, there was another knock on the door.

'Madame!' Rênal shouted. 'There are thieves in the house. A servant has found a ladder ouside your room! Open this door immediately!'

Julien tried to get off the bed, but Louise held him more closely.

'Oh, let him find us, Julien!' she said. 'Let him kill us! I don't want to go on living. I'll be happy if we die together tonight.'

But Julien did not want to die that night.

'No, madame,' he whispered. 'Think of your children.

'I'm tired and I need to sleep,' Louise said.

You mustn't leave them without a mother. I'll jump out of the window. Please throw my clothes down after me. Then open the door and talk to your husband while I get away. Goodbye, my love.'

Julien kissed Louise, and a moment later he had jumped down into the garden. When Louise threw his clothes down after him, Julien picked them up and ran towards the garden wall. As Julien ran, someone in the house fired a gun at him. None of the bullets hit Julien, but he quickly climbed over the wall and ran towards the River Doubs. He did not stop and put on his clothes until he reached the river.

An hour later, Julien was walking along the road which crosses the border between France and Switzerland.

'If the mayor and his servants are searching for me, they'll search on the Paris road,' the young man told himself. 'I'll be safe if I travel this way.'

10

Paris

When Julien Sorel finally arrived in Paris, Abbé Pirard met him.

'I'll take you to your new employer,' said the abbé. 'But before I do that, Julien, there are two things that I must explain. First, you must understand your position with the marquis. You are to be his secretary. You'll copy letters for him. You'll write to lawyers for him. You'll look after Monsieur de La Mole's property in many parts of the country. You'll have to travel sometimes.

'If you do all this work well,' continued Abbé Pirard, 'The marquis will begin to trust[93] you. When he trusts you, you'll

71

learn a lot about your employer's business. But you can only speak about his business with members of M. de La Mole's family, or his lawyers. The marquis has very many enemies. Probably, someone will ask you to spy on M. de La Mole. Someone will offer you a lot of money to talk about M. de La Mole's business. You mustn't be corrupted by these people, Julien. You must be honest with your employer.'

'I shall always be honest,' Julien replied.

'The second thing I have to explain is about your life with M. de La Mole,' the abbé went on. 'You'll live in his house and you'll be treated well. The marquis and his family know all about *your* family. They know that you're the son of a peasant and that you're trying to improve your life. But you won't live like a servant. In the evenings, you'll dine with the Mole family. You'll talk with them and their friends after dinner. You must try to please the Moles. They'll be kind to you. But remember this – M. de La Mole's family is very rich, but there is something more important to them than money. They are aristocrats. They have a lot of power. There have been members of the marquis's family in powerful positions in France for hundreds of years.'

'Yes, monsieur,' said Julien.

'Monsieur de La Mole and his family will behave politely and kindly towards you,' Abbé Pirard went on. 'You must be polite to them and work hard. Aristocrats will show good manners towards people who are below them in society. But remember this: If you don't serve them well, they will treat you with great contempt.'

'Yes, I understand,' Julien replied. 'But please tell me more about the family.'

'The Marquis de la Mole and his wife – the Marquise – have two children, a son and a daughter,' said Abbé Pirard. 'Mademoiselle Mathilde de La Mole – the marquis's daughter, is nineteen years old. She's a very proud young woman. I don't think that she'll say much to you. Her brother – Norbert, the Comte de La Mole – is a major in the army. He'll be kind and polite. But please remember, Julien, you *cannot* be a close friend of the count. And you'll *never* be his equal. You are the Marquis de La Mole's secretary. You must not forget this.'

———

Julien was taken to the grand house where the marquis and his family lived when they were in Paris. The room where he was going to sleep was large and its windows looked out onto a beautiful garden. Julien was given two new black suits and twenty shirts. And soon, he met his new employer in the enormous library.

When Julien had seen the Marquis de La Mole at Verrières, the aristocrat had seemed cold and unfriendly. But now he smiled at Julien. He told the young man what he had to do. The two men liked each other immediately and Julien was happy.

'I'll enjoy this new life,' Julien thought. 'I have a beautiful room and good clothes. The work will be interesting and I'll be able to save some money. M. de La Mole and his friends and family are all Ultras, so I must be careful. I must never say anything that shows my admiration for the Liberals or Napoleon. I must pretend to admire the King and the Church. If I remember all this, I'll enjoy the conversations at dinner. And I'll enjoy being here – for a while.'

Soon Julien found out that the Abbé Pirard had understood the Mole family very well. Everybody behaved as the abbé had guessed they would. Comte Norbert was friendly. The marquise and her daughter were polite, but they did not say much to the new secretary.

Sometimes, Julien made mistakes and he did things which showed his inexperience. Then, at dinner, these mistakes became jokes. For example, Julien's Latin was excellent. But his spelling was not always good when he was writing in French. One day, the marquis found some spelling mistakes in a letter which Julien had copied. And that evening, M. de La Mole made a joke about it at dinner. But it was not an unkind joke, and Julien was able to laugh at himself. A few minutes later, M. de La Mole started talking about the poet Horace. Abbé Pirard had told the marquis that Julien knew about this poet's work, and M. de La Mole remembered this. Julien was able to speak intelligently about Horace's poems. He recited some of them in Latin. And after that, even the ladies seemed to have more respect for the young secretary.

Julien realized that there were many things about life in the great city which he did not know.

'Listening to the Mole family talking together is strange,' he thought. 'It's like listening to a conversation in a foreign language – a language which I am still learning. I can understand what they say, but I can't speak the language.'

When Julien first went to Paris, Mademoiselle de La Mole was cold and unfriendly towards him. But Julien did not worry about that. He had soon realized that Abbé Pirard's words about her were true. Mathilde de La Mole was very proud and arrogant. Certainly, she was a beautiful young woman. She had lovely fair hair and wonderful blue eyes.

'But Louise de Rênal had wonderful eyes too,' Julien thought. 'And she is far away. But I still love her.'

———

Several months passed. Julien was a secretary to an aristocrat, but he was still studying to be a priest. Twice each week, he went to classes in a seminary which was near M. de La Mole's Parisian house. And Abbé Pirard also took him to meet some Jansenist priests who were his friends. Julien was surprised and impressed by the Jansenists. They were serious and pious men. They were not like the lazy, greedy priests Julien had met in the seminaries.

'Listening to the Mole family is like listening to a conversation
in a foreign language,' he thought.

Julien was now less interested in becoming a priest. He only wanted to work for M. de La Mole. Julien did this work well. He controlled many properties which belonged to the marquis. Most of these houses were in Brittany and Normandy – regions far to the west of Paris.

Julien often had to visit the marquis's properties. And sometimes, he met people who were part of his employer's political work. Once, Julien went to England to talk to some people who had been writing to M. de La Mole. Julien was good at listening to people and getting information from them. So the marquis sent his secretary to find out what these people really thought. When Julien returned to Paris, his employer questioned him for a long time.

'Monsieur Sorel, you've done very well,' the marquis said at last. 'You come to see me every morning, wearing the black clothes of a secretary. We work together. We talk about my business. You never tell me your own opinions. And that is good. That is how a secretary should behave. But today, my tailor will make a new coat for you. It will be made from fine blue cloth.

'Now I want to ask you something,' the marquis went on. 'From today, when your work is finished at the end of each afternoon, will you come and see me? And at these times, will you wear your blue coat? In the afternoons, you won't be my secretary, you'll be my young friend, Julien. We won't talk about business. We'll talk about other things. And you won't be a peasant's son from Verrières. In the afternoons, we'll pretend that you're the second son of an old friend of mine. We'll pretend that you are an aristocrat who I haven't seen for many years.'

After this, Julien visited the Marquis de La Mole almost every afternoon when he had finished his work. And soon the two men had become good companions. The marquis now trusted the strange young peasant completely.

11

Mathilde

Many rich young aristocrats visited M. de La Mole's house in the evenings. They were all friends of Comte Norbert and Mademoiselle Mathilde. When Julien listened to their conversations, he realized that these young men and women had no respect. They talked about other people and mocked[94] them. But the people who they mocked were always other aristocrats and very rich people. This surprised Julien.

One evening, Mathilde, Norbert and their friends talked about an important member of the government and they told jokes about him.

'Tonight, they're mocking the richest man in France,' Julien thought. 'They don't care what they say.'

Perhaps because these young people did not care what they said, Julien soon became a little careless too. Several of the aristocratic young men liked Mathilde. There were her admirers and they wanted to marry her. The Marquis de La Mole wanted Mathilde to marry a rich aristocrat from an old family, so he was happy when these young men came to the house. But Mathilde did not seem interested in them. She thought they were a little boring. However, there was one young man who was not like the others. He was not French, he was Italian. And he was a Jansenist and a Liberal. The young man was living in France because he could not live in his own country. The Italian government wanted to execute him.

One evening, Julien and the young Italian began to talk about Napoleon. After several minutes, Julien forgot about being careful. He gave his own opinions. The young Italian agreed with Julien's opinions and both men became excited.

Suddenly Julien realized that Mathilde had been listening to their conversation.

She laughed. 'I didn't know that our young student priest admired Bonaparte,' she said to the Italian.

For several days, Julien was worried. Would Mathilde tell her father what she had heard? Would the marquis dismiss him? But M. de La Mole said nothing about Julien's opinions on Napoleon. And soon Julien had something else to think about. He had found out a secret about Mathilde de La Mole.

Mathilde often came into the library where Julien worked and borrowed her father's books. When she took a book from a shelf, she moved all the other books closer together. Julien watched her do this several times. At last he found out which books Mathilde was reading. She was reading books about the Revolution. And she was reading books by Liberals.

The truth was this: Mathilde liked a little danger in her life. Although she was a proud aristocrat, she thought that the idea of revolution was exciting. When she thought about the things that had happened to the aristocrats during the Revolution, she was excited. Now she knew that Julien and the young Italian Jansenist admired Napoleon. She found that exciting too. Almost all the men that she knew were Ultras. And they were lazy and boring.

'All my admirers are like my brother,' she said to herself. 'They don't have opinions of their own. But the Revolutionaries did have thoughts and opinions of their own.'

Mathilde was interested in books which were written by people who were against the French king. This was one reason why she often went to the library. And the other reason for her visits? She went to look at Julien. Why? Because she had decided that she was in love with him!

Mathilde was now nineteen years old and she had never loved a man. She wanted to fall in love with a man and she wanted to be loved by a man. She wanted a lover. But why had she decided to love Julien Sorel? He was her father's secretary and the son of a peasant! One reason was that she was very proud. She did not want an ordinary love affair. She wanted a Grand Passion[95].

'Julien is a simple person,' she told herself. 'I couldn't love him if he was simple and rich. If Julien had money, my father might think that he was a suitable husband for me. But that wouldn't be a Grand Passion, that would be boring. Julien isn't a rich, simple person. He's a simple person with no money at all. He is *not* a suitable person for me, so I'll love him. He's intelligent and I'm rich. With my help, he could be anything and do anything. I'll help him!'

However, the thing that Mathilde liked most about Julien was his pride. She had realized that he was as proud as she was.

When Julien had arrived at the house, Mathilde had not spoken to him. She had shown her contempt for the student priest. And she had wanted Julien to be upset by all this. But he had not been upset. In fact, Julien had shown Mathilde that he did not care about her thoughts. He had shown her that he was not interested in her money, or her pride, or her rich friends. He was too proud to notice her contempt. Mathilde guessed that if there was another revolution in France, Julien would be one of the leaders. He would happily send her and her family to the guillotine!

And because of all this, she decided that she loved him!

———

At first, Julien did not realize what had happened. One day – it was the thirtieth of April – Julien noticed that Mathilde was dressed in black clothes. She wore black clothes all that day. She wore black clothes at dinner too. Julien asked one of her friends about this.

'Mademoiselle Mathilde de La Mole always wears black on the thirtieth of April,' the young man replied. 'She does it because one of her ancestors died on that day, in 1574. Her ancestor's name was Boniface de La Mole. Boniface was the lover of Marguerite of Navarre. Marguerite's husband was King Henri IV. One of Boniface's enemies betrayed him, and Boniface was arrested[96]. He was executed on 30th April, 1574. After the execution, Marguerite of Navarre took her lover's head and she buried it in the ground. Mathilde de La Mole has always admired Marguerite's behaviour on that day.'

Julien hated the pride of these aristocrats. But he thought that this story from the sixteenth century was wonderful. He understood why Mathilde felt very proud of her ancestors.

A few days later, Julien told Mathilde that he knew the story about Boniface de La Mole and Marguerite of Navarre.

'What brave people they were!' he said.

'Yes,' Mathilde replied. 'Marguerite's love for Boniface was true love. I hope that, one day, I'll love someone like that.'

Then Mathilde told Julien all about her feelings for her ancestors. And he told her more about his feelings for his hero, Napoleon. He now felt quite safe when he talked about his admiration for Napoleon. And after that, Julien and Mathilde spent more and more time together.

'Mademoiselle de La Mole always wears black on
the thirtieth of April.'

12

In Love Again

Soon, Julien guessed that Mathilde was in love with him. At first, he thought that this was strange.

'Why is she interested in me?' he asked himself. He did not understand Mathilde, so he could not answer his own question. 'Perhaps I should make her my mistress. I believe that is what she wants. And she's certainly a beautiful young woman. I don't love her, because I still love Louise de Rênal. But I don't think that I'll ever meet Louise again. And I would like to have another love affair.

'But if Mathilde becomes my mistress, her father might find out about it,' Julien said to himself. 'Monsieur de La Mole would be angry. I don't want that to happen. He has certainly been very kind to me, and I enjoy my work here. I don't want the marquis and the marquise to be upset.'

So Julien made a decision and he chose the right way to behave. But then he changed his mind.

'Everyone has to make their own success,' Julien told himself. 'Why should I – a poor man who admires Napoleon – care about this family of rich aristocrats? If Mathilde asks me to be her lover, I'll agree.'

Julien wanted Mathilde to be his mistress, but he would not ask her. He was too proud.

'What *are* her true feelings?' he asked himself. 'Perhaps she'll laugh at me. Then I wouldn't be able to stay here. I'd have to leave Paris.'

So the two young people watched each other and said nothing. They were both too proud to speak to each other about their feelings.

It was Mathilde who spoke about her feelings first. She believed that she was in love. After weeks of unhappiness, she wrote a letter to Julien. In the letter, Mathilde told Julien that she loved him. She told him that she needed to see him alone.

Julien wrote a reply to Mathilde. He said that he was happy that she loved him. And he asked how and when they could meet secretly. Soon after this, he had another letter from her. This letter said:

Go into the garden at one o'clock tonight. There's a ladder on the ground under my window. The servants have left it there. Put the ladder against the wall of the house and climb up to my room. My window will be open.

When Julien read this letter, he was very excited. But then he thought about Mathilde's invitation more carefully. He began to worry. Suddenly, he was suspicious about his visit to Mathilde's room.

'Does Mathilde really love me?' he asked himself. 'Or does she want to mock me? Will she lock her window, look through the glass, and laugh at me? Or does she want to punish me? Her father or her brother might catch me while I'm trying to get into her room. Does Mathilde want this to happen? Does she want me to be sent away? Or does she want the servants to kill me? If the moon is bright tonight, anyone could see me climbing up to her window.'

And then he thought again.

'If I go into the garden tonight, I'll take Mathilde's letter with me,' he told himself. 'Then, if I'm caught, I'll show the letter to everyone. The letter will prove[97] that I'm doing what Mathilde wants me to do.'

A moment later, Julien thought of something else.

'But what if a servant catches me in the garden? The servant might take the letter and destroy it. Then I'll have no proof of Mathilde's invitation.'

Finally, Julien decided that he would visit Mathilde. But he made a plan to protect himself.

He put both of Mathilde's letters into an envelope. Then he wrote the address of his friend, Fouqué, on the envelope. He also wrote this message on it:

If you hear that I've been killed or arrested, open this envelope. Make copies of the letters that are inside and send them to the newspapers.
Julien Sorel

After writing this, Julien sent the envelope to Fouqué's house in the mountains.

———

At one o'clock in the morning, Julien entered the garden and found the ladder. He looked all round the garden, but saw no one. Carefully, he put the ladder against the wall of the house and climbed up to the window of Mathilde's room.

The window was open and she was waiting for him inside the room. A moment later, Julien had climbed through the open window and Mathilde was in his arms.

'She really does love me!' Julien thought happily. 'I was foolish to be suspicious!'

But as soon as Julien held her in his arms, Mathilde became very worried.

'Why have I done this?' she thought. 'Do I really want this peasant boy to be my lover?'

'Julien, do you have my letters?' she asked him. 'Will you give them to me?'

When he heard this, Julien quickly became suspicious again.

'She *is* trying to destroy me!' he thought. 'When she has the letters, she'll call her father. She'll pretend that she never invited me here.'

84

She was waiting for him inside the room.

'No, my darling Mathilde, you can't have the letters,' Julien replied. 'I've sent them to my friend in another town. The letters will be safe with him. I'll get them when I visit him again. I'll get the letters then, unless something terrible happens to me before that.'

Julien spoke quite loudly when he said this.

'If a servant is hiding in this room, he'll have heard my words,' Julien thought. 'No one will attack me now. I'll be safe because I have Mathilde's letters. I'll be safe, even if Mathilde's brother and father are hiding here.'

So Julien looked suspiciously at Mathilde, and Mathilde looked suspiciously at Julien. At first, they were both so suspicious of each other, that neither of them could think about romance.

———

Before that night ended, Julien and Mathilde had become lovers.

When the sun rose, Julien left Mathilde's room. She was now his mistress. But he did not begin to feel happy about this until he was in his own room.

'Perhaps I do love her,' he told himself. 'She's very brave and she's very beautiful. Yes, I do love Mathilde de La Mole. I won't think about Louise de Rênal again. Perhaps a new life is beginning for me now.'

But at the same time, Mathilde was lying in her own room and she was thinking sad thoughts.

'Perhaps I was wrong,' she thought. 'Perhaps I don't love Julien Sorel. He's my father's servant … and he's a peasant. And now he'll think that he's my master. That must not happen!'

13

A Strange Mission[98]

Later that morning, when Julien saw Mathilde walking towards him in the garden, he was happy. He wanted to tell his new mistress how much he loved her. But this did not happen. Mathilde was scornful and proud. Once again, she was a rich young aristocrat who was talking to her father's secretary. And Julien was a peasant's son from Verrières.

'I made a mistake last night, monsieur,' she told him angrily. 'Perhaps you think that you're my master now. But you're wrong! And if you're not a completely bad person, you'll forget everything about last night.'

When he heard these words, Julien's pride returned too.

'I'll never speak of last night to you, or to anyone,' he replied coldly. 'I can promise you that, mademoiselle.'

For many weeks, Julien and Mathilde did not speak to each other. And they were both very unhappy.

'Well, perhaps she loved me for a week or two,' thought Julien. 'She doesn't love me now. But I'll always love her.'

'The little peasant is so cold and proud,' thought Mathilde. 'I'm sure that he would kill me, if he could. But I was wrong about him. I do love him! He's so strong!'

Neither lover wanted to be the first one to speak about their feelings. There was a war of pride between them. But at last, they were both so unhappy that one of them had to speak.

If Mathilde had spoken first, everything might have been all right between them. But it was Julien who started the conversation. They met in the library.

'Ah, don't you love me now?' he said sadly. 'I love you so much.'

Mathilde had been going to say the same words herself. But when she heard Julien say them, all her love disappeared again.

'He's so weak!' she thought. 'I can't love someone who lets me win a battle so easily.'

And so the war of pride continued.

———

After several more weeks of unhappiness, Julien made a decision. He was walking in the garden late one night. Everyone else had gone to bed.

'I'll leave Paris tomorrow,' he decided. 'The Marquis de La Mole has been kind to me, but I can't stay in his house any longer. I love Mathilde, but she behaves like a stupid, proud child.'

As Julien thought about everything that had happened to him, his sadness disappeared. He became angry. He arrived below Mathilde's window and his feeling of anger grew stronger.

'She must be awake,' he thought. 'A light is still burning in her room.'

And by the light that came from the window, Julien saw that the ladder was still on the ground.

Suddenly Julien remembered his last visit to Verrières. He had climbed a ladder to Louise's room then, but she had not wanted to see him. Louise had tried to send Julien away. But he had stayed, and he had enjoyed the most wonderful twenty-four hours of his life!

Julien looked around M. de La Mole's garden. He did not really care if anyone saw him. He picked up the ladder and put it against the wall of the house. He climbed the ladder quickly and knocked loudly on Mathilde's window. In a moment, he saw his lover's face behind the glass.

'Let me in, Mathilde!' he said angrily. 'Stop behaving like a foolish child! Let me in!'

Mathilde saw the anger on Julien's face and heard the anger in his voice. And suddenly, after weeks of unhappiness, she was full of joy again.

'I was wrong! Julien isn't weak!' she thought. 'He's strong! Yes, he *is* my master.'

She opened the window and pulled Julien into the room. And that night there was no hate between them. There was only love.

───

One evening a few days later, the Marquis de La Mole asked Julien to meet him in the library. He asked the young man to sit down, and he gave him a newspaper.

'Abbé Pirard has told me that you have an excellent memory, Julien,' the marquis said. 'Now I wish to test your memory. I want you to read and remember the first page of this newspaper. Please try to memorize every word. I'll leave this room for half an hour. When I return, I want you to recite every word that you have learned. Then I'll know how good your memory is.'

The marquis left the room and Julien did what he had been asked to do.

When M. de La Mole returned to the library, Julien gave him the newspaper. Then he recited every word from the first page. While Julien recited perfectly, his employer looked at the paper in front of him and checked every word.

'That is excellent, Julien,' said the marquis when the young man had finished. 'And now I'll explain why I needed to test your memory. I'm going to send you on an important mission.

'In a few minutes,' M. de La Mole continued, 'we're going to leave this house. We will travel in my carriage to a secret meeting in another part of the city. There'll be some very important people at this meeting. You must never talk about what you see or hear. You'll see aristocrats, generals from the army, and politicians at the meeting. And you'll also see leaders of the Church – bishops and important Jesuits.

'When we arrive, I'll introduce you,' the marquis went on. 'I'll tell them that you're my secretary. After that, you'll say nothing. But you'll listen very carefully to everything that you hear. And you'll take notes about everything. It will probably be quite a long meeting, and you'll have to write many pages of notes. After the meeting has finished, we'll return to this library. Then we'll work together. We'll look at your notes. We'll decide which of the things that were said at the meeting are most important.

'When we've made our decisions, we'll write a summary of your notes,' M. de La Mole said. 'We'll write those most important points on only a few pages. And when we've done *that*, you'll memorize that summary, Julien. When you've memorized the summary, I'll destroy all the written notes. Tomorrow, I'll send you on a journey to meet another very important person. And that man will be the most important person you will *ever* meet. You'll have to recite to him the summary that you've memorized. Do you understand me?'

'Yes, monsieur,' Julien replied. 'I'm proud that you trust me. I'll be proud to go on this mission for you. But where am I going? And who am I going to recite the summary to?'

'I'll answer those questions tomorrow,' the marquis replied.

———

Everything the marquis had told Julien about the meeting was correct.

The important people talked about politics. They all wanted to make sure that France would always be ruled by a king. They had many different suggestions about how to do this. The generals wanted the French army to kill people. The bishops wanted more power to be given to the Church. The aristocrats wanted to have armies of their own. They wanted the peasants who worked on their land to become soldiers. But everyone had one thought that was the same. Nobody in the meeting wanted another revolution.

Julien did exactly what he had been told to do. Nobody could have guessed that the young secretary was a Bonapartist. And nobody could have guessed that he hated these Ultras and their politics.

Before dawn the next morning, Julien was again sitting with Monsieur de La Mole in his library. The two men looked at the notes that Julien had written after the secret meeting. Then they made a summary of these notes. Next, the marquis tested Julien's memory. He asked him to recite the summary which he had learned by heart. After that, M. de La Mole destroyed all the papers from the meeting.

'Julien, your mission will be dangerous,' the marquis said. 'Only one other person must know what was discussed last night. No one else must know. This is most important. That's why I asked you to memorize the summary. If you're attacked, no one can steal any written notes because there aren't any.'

'And *will* someone try to attack me, monsieur?' asked Julien.

'Not everyone at that meeting last night was an honest man,' the marquis told Julien. 'At least two people didn't believe what they were saying. They'll probably try to stop your mission. Before you reach the man who you're going to meet, these two men might try to kill you. So you must be very careful on your journey.'

'And where am I going, monsieur?' asked Julien. 'Will you tell me that now?'

'You're going Strasbourg, my young friend,' M. de La Mole replied.

Nobody could have guessed that the young secretary hated these Ultras and their politics.

14
A New Life

A few hours later, the Marquis de La Mole and Julien left Paris and travelled many miles south of the city. They went to a country house which belonged to the marquis. From the house, Julien was going to travel onwards alone. He was given a small carriage and official documents with a false name. He was also given some new clothes. Now, instead of a simple black secretary's suit, Julien was wearing colourful and expensive clothes. He looked like a very rich young man. More clothes of this kind were in his travelling cases.

'Julien, when you stop at an inn for the night, you must pretend to be a bored, rich young traveller,' said M. de La Mole. 'Don't answer *any* questions about where you are travelling and why. Your documents will allow you to enter the towns of Metz and Strasbourg. But don't show the papers to anyone on your journey unless you are arrested.'

'Am I going to enter Metz, monsieur?' Julien asked.

'Yes,' the marquis replied. 'Before you go to Strasbourg, you must go to Metz. You must go there to meet the man that I spoke about. I couldn't tell you this before. But now you must know everything.'

Then the marquis told Julien who he was going to meet. He was going to meet a man who was a famous and very clever politician from a foreign country. And the man was also a prince.

'We need the prince's advice,' M. de La Mole said. 'He doesn't want another revolution in France. You must go to the prince's house in Metz – I'll tell you how to find it. You must recite to him the summary that you have memorized. Then you'll travel on to Strasbourg and wait there for a week. When the prince has had time to think about our problem, you must visit him again. He'll give you a reply. You must memorize his words. After this, you must return to Paris and repeat them to me. Return as quickly as possible. You mustn't write any notes.'

'But will the prince trust me, monsieur?' Julien asked. 'How will he know that I'm working for you?'

The Marquis de La Mole took a watch from his pocket.

'Take this watch and give me your own watch,' he replied. 'When you see the prince, show him my watch. He'll recognize it.'

Then M. de La Mole tested Julien's memory again. He asked Julien to recite the summary one more time. And when he said goodbye to the young man, the marquis gave him one more thing – a gun.

'I hope that you won't need to use it,' he said.

———

Two days later, Julien arrived at a village near the town of Metz. The horses that were pulling Julien's carriage were tired and he needed some fresh ones. Julien asked the owner of an inn if he could borrow fresh horses. But the innkeeper told him that there were no extra horses in the village.

'You'll have to stay here tonight,' the innkeeper said. 'I'm sorry that you have been delayed. Perhaps I'll be able to get fresh horses for you tomorrow. Then you can continue your journey. May I ask you where you are going next, monsieur?'

'Oh, I don't know. I haven't decided,' Julien replied. He spoke slowly. He was pretending to be bored. 'But I can't believe that there are no extra horses here,' he added. 'Are you sure that you can't find fresh horses for me?'

'Yes, I'm quite sure, monsieur,' the man replied. 'You can look in my stables. They are empty today.'

Later in the afternoon, Julien went for a walk. He met a boy in the street. He gave the boy some money and asked him some questions.

'Are you sure that you can't find fresh horses for me?'

'Have you seen anything strange here today?' Julien asked the boy.

'Well, something strange happened this morning,' the boy replied. 'There were ten or twelve horses in the stables at the inn. But at midday, every horse was moved to a second stable at the other end of the village. The innkeeper has been asked to delay a secret messenger. That is what someone told me.'

When Julien returned to the inn, he said nothing to the innkeeper. But when the man brought Julien a large glass of wine with his evening meal, Julien did not drink it. He threw the wine out of the window. Then he went to bed.

———

In the middle of the night, Julien awoke suddenly. He had heard a noise. There were two people in his room and one of them was holding a lighted candle. By the candle's light, Julien saw the innkeeper standing in the centre of the room. The second man was a priest who was wearing long dark robes. He was looking in Julien's travelling cases.

'Search the cases carefully,' the innkeeper said. 'You won't wake the young man. I put a drug in his wine. He'll sleep all night and all day.'

'You did well,' the priest replied. 'But I think that this is the wrong young man. The clothes in these cases belong to a rich young traveller. This isn't the messenger from Paris who we were expecting. This isn't the spy that the bishop told me about.'

When he heard these words, Julien thought about the men at the secret meeting in Paris. He quickly guessed which bishop had arranged this delay. And then Julien thought about the gun which was hidden in his bed. He wanted to shoot the men, but he had to think about his mission.

'If I kill them, I'll have to stay in this village and answer questions,' he told himself. 'I must not be delayed any longer.'

So Julien pretended to be asleep, and the innkeeper and the priest left the room. A few minutes later, Julien got out of bed and left the inn very quietly. At the other end of the village, he found the second stable and took some horses. Half an hour later, they were pulling his carriage towards Metz.

———

Julien arrived in Metz very early the next day. He went immediately to the prince's house. But the prince's servants would not let Julien enter the house. So he waited in the street until the early evening.

Suddenly, the door of the house opened and the prince came out. Julien recognized the prince immediately. He had seen pictures of him in newspapers. The prince started to walk down the street. In a moment, Julien was walking beside him. He took M. de La Mole's watch from his pocket.

The prince did not stop walking. But as he walked, he spoke quietly to Julien. 'Follow me, monsieur,' he said, 'but stay twenty metres behind me.'

After he had followed the prince for ten minutes, Julien saw him enter a small café. Julien entered the café too. The prince was sitting in a dark corner. He pointed to a chair next to him, and Julien sat down.

'What is your message, monsieur?' the great man asked.

Julien recited the summary which he had memorized. When he had finished, the prince spoke again.

'Please repeat everything that you have said, but speak much more slowly this time,' he told Julien.

This time, the prince wrote notes while Julien recited his summary. When the prince had finished writing, he spoke again.

'Thank you, monsieur,' he said. 'Now listen to me. Today you must travel to Strasbourg. Leave your carriage here and borrow a horse. Ride to Strasbourg, wait there for one week and then return to Metz. In ten days' time, come to this café at the same hour of the day. Then I'll give you a reply for M.

'In ten days' time, come to this café at the same hour of the day. Then I'll give you a reply for M. de La Mole and his friends.'

de La Mole and his friends. I'll leave this café now, but you must stay here for half an hour. No one must see us together in the street.'

———

While Julien waited in Strasbourg, he thought a lot about Mathilde. He was sure that he loved her very much. Julien did not know what was going to happen in the future. But he felt that a new life had started for him.

When Julien met the prince again, he was given an answer for M. de La Mole. Julien memorized this answer and then he started his journey back to Paris. This time, there were no delays and no difficulties. As soon as he arrived at the Marquis de La Mole's house, Julien recited the prince's words to his employer. Then he went to find Mathilde.

The two young people met in the library.

'Julien, I must tell you something,' Mathilde said happily. 'I'm pregnant – I'm going to have a baby. I'm going to have your child!'

15

Guilt and Revenge

The next day, Mathilde de La Mole wrote a letter to her father.

My dear father
I've something to tell you. I'm going to have a baby. The father of the child is Julien Sorel. I love Julien very much and I want to marry him. I know that you'll be upset by this news. You've always wanted me to marry an aristocrat and become a marquise. But I love Julien and I will not marry anyone else.

Will you be kind to us, Father? Will you give Julien and me some money? Then we can live together in the way that you want your daughter to live. If you want this to happen, we'll marry soon. Then I'll leave Paris and go to the country. I'll stay there until my baby is born.

If you won't give us any money and allow us to marry, Julien and I will go to Switzerland. We'll live together there. Julien will become a teacher of Latin and literature. He's very clever and he'll do well. I'll be with him and I'll be happy.

Of course, it will be better if you let us marry because then I can go on seeing you. I don't know what you will decide to do. But I must be with Julien.

Father, please don't blame Julien for what has happened. I fell in love with him and I told him this. I made him love me. If anyone must be blamed, it is myself. Please remember this.

Your loving daughter,
Mathilde

When M. de La Mole read this letter, he was very angry. He sent for Julien and shouted at him. The marquis said some terrible things to his secretary. But he could not believe that the young man was really bad. And after a while, the marquis became quieter.

'Monsieur,' Julien said quietly, 'I know that you've been good to me. You think that I've behaved badly and you think that I'm ungrateful. But the truth is this: Your daughter and I are lovers. We are expecting a child. I love your daughter very much. And I want to care for my child.'

'Oh, I know that Mathilde is strong and proud,' M. de La Mole replied more kindly. 'But when you realized that she had fallen in love with you, you *should* have left my house immediately,' the marquis said sadly. 'Well, you must leave now – immediately! I need some time to think. But you cannot work for me any longer. Go to Abbé Pirard and stay with him. I'll send you some money for your food and clothes. But don't come to this house again, monsieur!'

———

The Marquis de La Mole was a very changeable person. In the weeks that followed, he changed his mind many times. He made dozens of decisions, and then he thought of dozens of different decisions.

At last, he decided that he needed more information about Julien. This son of a peasant was the father of his daughter's baby. He wanted to know more about the young man's family. So the marquis wrote some letters to Verrières.

A week later, Julien received a note from Mathilde.

My darling Julien
Something terrible has happened. I must see you today. Come in a carriage and meet me in the street behind my father's house at two o'clock. I love you.

Julien did what Mathilde asked. At two o'clock he found her waiting for him in the street behind the marquis's house. Julien jumped out of the carriage and ran to meet her.

'What has happened?' he asked.

'Oh, my darling. My father won't let me marry you,' Mathilde replied. 'He's received this dreadful letter.'

She held out the letter to show him. 'My father gave it to me,' Mathilde said. 'He told me to read it and said, "Now you'll see what kind of man Monsieur Julien Sorel really is." We must run away together, Julien. We must go to Switzerland.'

Julien looked at the letter. He recognized the handwriting – it was Louise de Rênal's. He started to read it. His hands were shaking with fear.

Monsieur

I have to be honest with you. And I must do this for God and the Church.

You wrote to ask me about M. Julien Sorel, the young man who is your secretary. I must warn you about this man. He's a bad, cruel person. It's painful for me to say this, but it's true.

Julien Sorel is a peasant's son who is trying to make money and get power. But to do this, M. Sorel betrays weak women. He gets work in the houses of important and respected men. If a woman in the house can help him with his career, he pretends to fall in love with her. No man should introduce M. Sorel to his wife, or to his daughter.

'Poor Louise,' Julien thought. 'She's feeling guilty again. Abbé Pirard told me that there is a new curé in Verrières who is very pious. I'm sure that when Louise received M. de La Mole's letter, she felt guilty. She went to the church in Verrières and told the new curé about our love affair. I'm sure that the new curé made her write this terrible letter.'

Then Julien felt angry. 'Louise doesn't love me any more,' he thought. 'But she wants to stop anyone else loving me!'

This is what Julien thought. But when he spoke to Mathilde there was no anger in his voice.

'Your father is an honest man and he's respected,' Julien said. 'I don't blame him for writing to Mme de Rênal. And no father would want his daughter to marry the kind of man who is described in this letter. Goodbye, Mathilde.'

As soon as he had finished speaking, Julien ran back to his carriage and jumped into it. A few moments later he was travelling towards Verrières. He still had the gun which he had taken to Strasbourg.

———

It was Sunday morning when Julien arrived in Verrières. He entered the church and saw Louise de Rênal sitting in a seat

Then he lifted the gun and shot her.

near the front of the church. For a few seconds, he looked at the woman who he had loved so deeply. Then he lifted the gun and shot her.

Then Julien dropped the gun and turned to walk away. But everyone in the church was shouting, and there were strong men between him and the door. A few moments later, Julien had been arrested.

16

Prison

J ulien Sorel sat in a cell in the prison at Verrières. He had been locked in this small room for several days. Julien had been arrested for the crime[99] of murder.

That morning, Julien had written a short message to Mathilde:

I've taken my revenge. I've killed the person who told your father lies about me. Goodbye, my dear. Be kind to our child, but forget about me. Forget that I ever lived.

'I killed Louise, and I should die,' Julien thought. 'Soon there'll be a trial. The trial won't take a long time because I'll tell everyone that I'm guilty. And in a few weeks' time, I'll be taken to the guillotine and executed. And that will be the end of my life. Will that be so bad?'

Julien remembered a famous leader of the Jacobins who had been executed by his enemies.

'Before the Jacobin died, he made a clever joke to the gaoler[100] in his prison,' Julien said to himself. 'The leader of the Jacobins told the gaoler, "It's impossible to use the past tense of the verb *to be guillotined* with the pronoun *I*. You can say, *I'm going to be guillotined*. And perhaps you can even say,

I'm being guillotined. But you can never say, *I have been guillotined!*" '

Later, Julien thought about his own death.

'There'll be many people watching me die,' he said to himself. 'I hope that I'll be as brave as the Jacobite leader. Will I die bravely? Perhaps I'll throw some money to the crowd. Perhaps I'll make a speech.'

But then Julien realized another thing. After his death, he would not have to behave like an actor! He would not have to be careful how he behaved. He would not have to think carefully about the words that he spoke.

That afternoon, Julien received some strange news. One of the gaolers came to Julien's cell.

'Madame de Rênal isn't dead,' the goaler said. 'She was badly hurt, but you didn't kill her. She isn't going to die. She's getting better each day.'

Louise had also sent some money to the prison, but the gaoler did not tell Julien this.

Julien was being treated well. He was being given good food and wine. This money was the reason why Julien was being treated well. Louise had bribed[101] the gaolers.

When he heard the news about Louise, Julien was very happy.

'Louise used to love me,' he thought. 'And I loved her. I *was* trying to kill her, so I should die. But I'm glad that she isn't going to die too.'

At that moment, Julien started to believe in God. He believed that God had saved him from killing Louise de Rênal – the woman that he had loved. And then Julien knew that he still loved Louise. And as he thought this, he felt warm tears running down his face.

The next day, Julien was taken from the prison in Verrières to the prison in Besançon. His trial was going to take place in that town.

———

Julien's first visitor at Besançon was his old friend, Fouqué. Julien cried out when his friend entered the cell. The two men put their arms around each other and wept.

'Julien, I must help you,' Fouqué said. 'You can have all my money. We can use it to pay for good lawyers at your trial. And we can bribe the gaolers with it. If you are found guilty at your trial, you'll come back to this cell before your execution. You must get away from this prison and from Franche-Comté. We'll have to bribe the gaolers. We'll pay them to let you escape.'

'My friend, you're very kind,' Julien said to Fouqué. 'But I don't need money. And I won't try to escape. But please visit me again. I'm happy when I see you. Perhaps you can do something for me, before the end.'

The next day, Mathilde de La Mole started visiting Julien. She had heard about what had happened in Verrières. She had travelled from Paris and she was now staying in Besançon. On her first visit to the prison, Mathilde wore a disguise. She was not wearing her own clothes. She came to Julien's cell dressed in the clothes of a peasant. But nobody believed that Mathilde was a peasant because she bribed the gaolers with too much money. After a few days, she took off her disguise. She wore her own beautiful, colourful clothes.

At first Julien was not happy to see Mathilde. He had hoped that she would stay away from him.

'I told you to forget me, Mathilde,' he said. 'I don't want people to know that we were lovers. Listen to me! When I'm dead, you'll marry a fine, rich young man. That is what I want you to do. But your husband will not want the child of a peasant in his family. When our baby is born – and I believe that the child will be a boy – will you give him to Mme de Rênal? Will you let her keep him and care for him?'

'Louise de Rênal – the woman who you tried to kill?'

Mathilde said. She was shocked and surprised. 'The woman who wrote that terrible letter about you? You want *her* to take care of your son?'

'It will be best for him,' Julien told her gently. 'Mathilde, in fifteen years from now, you'll have forgotten me. And you'll have forgotten my son. You and your husband will have children of your own. But I believe that Mme de Rênal will take care of my child very well. And she will love him as much as she loves her own children.'

Mathilde was unhappy when she heard Julien's words. She wept. She held Julien in her arms and she told him that she loved him. She told him that she was going to get the best lawyers for him. She told Julien that he would soon be free.

'Madame de Rênal didn't die,' she said. 'At your trial, you must tell everyone that you weren't trying to kill her. Tell the court that it was an accident. No one can prove that you wanted Mme de Rênal to die.'

———

Mathilde visited Julien every day. Each day, she had a new plan for Julien's escape. However, she never made a decision to follow any of these plans. After a week, Julien was bored with Mathilde. He tried not to show his feelings. He tried to be kind to her. But now he only thought about Louise de Rênal.

———

Julien's trial was very strange. His lawyer spoke very well. He told the court that Julien had made a mistake when he fired the gun. The lawyer explained that it had been an accident. Julien had *not* been trying to kill Mme de Rênal. And the lawyer reminded everyone that Louise de Rênal was *alive*.

'Monsieur Julien Sorel is a clever young man of twenty-three,' said the lawyer. 'He has all of his life before him. He didn't go to the church to find the mayor's wife and kill her.

107

My dear sirs, it will be a crime and a sin if this innocent young man is executed.'

But Julien knew that his end was near. No one in the court had listened to the lawyer's words. Many of the men in the court were rich merchants from Verrières. They were men who knew Julien and they hated him. And these men were going to decide if Julien was guilty of the crime. One of the men was Valenod, the jealous merchant who had written anonymous letters to M. de Rênal. So when Julien spoke, he disagreed with his own lawyer.

'My lawyer is wrong,' he said. 'You're all rich men. You'll never understand the thoughts of a peasant like me. So I'm going to make your work easier. I say this: I *was* trying to murder Mme de Rênal. I wanted to kill her. I'm guilty, so I must die! That is all I have to say.'

The court decided that Julien was guilty. Now he knew that he *was* going to die. When he was taken back to the prison at Besançon, he was put in a small cold cell that had no windows.

––––

The day after the trial, Julien had three visitors. His father was the first visitor. Old Sorel shouted at Julien. He said cruel things to his youngest son. The old man had come to the prison to ask how much money he would get when Julien died. When he knew the answer to this question, old Sorel was quite happy.

'I won't come here again,' he said. And he left the prison.

The second visitor was Mathilde.

'You must ask the King of France to help you, my darling,' she told Julien. 'Only the king can stop your execution. The lawyer has written a letter to the king. He has told him all about your trial and he's asking the king to help you. The lawyer will bring the letter here tomorrow. You must sign the letter immediately.'

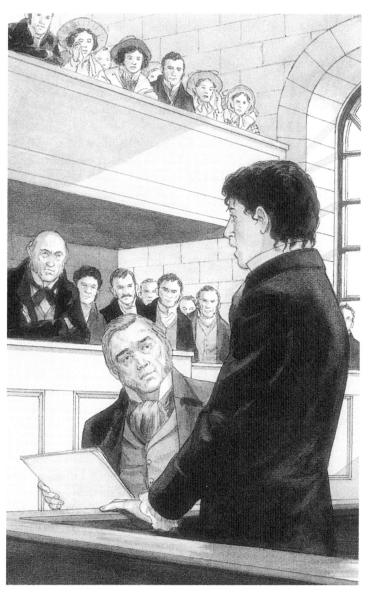

'I'm guilty, so I must die!'

'That won't help me, Mathilde,' Julien answered. 'I'm going to die. The letter might delay my execution, but I *will* have to go to the guillotine. I know that I'll have to wait for two months in this horrible cell before I have a reply from the king. This is my choice: I can wait for two months before I die, or I can die tomorrow. I'm tired. It will be much better for me to die tomorrow.'

When she heard Julien say this, Mathilde was angry.

'You won't even try to live for me and for our child!' she shouted. And for the rest of her visit, Mathilde behaved with coldness and contempt. She was once more a proud aristocrat!

After Mathilde had left his cell, Julien lay down and went to sleep. He awoke when he felt someone touch his shoulder. At first, Julien thought that Mathilde had returned to the cell. But when he opened his eyes, he saw Louise de Rênal standing beside him. He jumped up from his bed.

'Madame!' he said. 'I thank God that you're still alive!'

A moment later, Louise was holding Julien in her arms and tears were running down both their faces. They were tears of love.

'Ah Julien, you're here because of me!' Louise said. 'When you left me and went to Paris, I wanted to die. I hoped that I would become ill and die. But I didn't want to kill myself because that is a sin against God.

'The new curé of the church in Verrières told me to write that letter to M. de La Mole,' she continued. 'I was weak and very unhappy. I didn't know what I was doing. I did what he told me. And now you're here. If you die because of what I have done, I won't be able to live. My darling, I won't live for more than three days after you are dead.'

Julien and Louise talked together for several hours. They were happy. Now they knew that they loved each other deeply. Their love was a Grand Passion.

Before she left the cell, Louise asked Julien a question.

'Are you going to ask the king to help you?'

'Why must I live another two months in this cell?' he replied. 'At the end of that time, I *will* be executed. I know that. And my last sixty days in the world would have been very unhappy. If I die tomorrow, it will be after just one day of great happiness.'

'But if I visit you twice every day for those two months, your last sixty days might be as happy as today,' Louise said. 'Then after those sixty days, we'll both die.'

'Madame,' said Julien. 'I'll make a promise to you. If you will come to see me every day, I'll write to the king. I'll look forward to sixty more days with you before I die. And those sixty days will be the best days of my life. But you must make a promise to me. You must promise not to kill yourself after my death. You must promise not to make yourself ill. You must promise to live so that you can take care of my son.'

And Louise de Rênal promised.

17

The End

Louise de Rênal told her husband that she was leaving his house. She went to live with her rich aunt in Besançon so that she could visit Julien twice each day.

Mathilde visited Julien every day too. He always tried to be kind to Mathilde, but he only wanted to see Louise. Mathilde understood this and she was angry and jealous. But she loved Julien and she did not stop visiting him.

A few days before his execution, Fouqué visited Julien.

'My good friend,' Julien said. 'There are two things that I

want you to do for me. The first thing is this: At the time of my execution tomorrow, please take Mlle de La Mole and Mme de Rênal to another town. I don't want them to be here when I die. After my death, they'll no longer be jealous of each other. I hope that they'll help each other when I'm dead. Perhaps one day, they'll like each other.

'The second thing that I want you to do is this,' Julien went on. 'There's a little cave in the side of a mountain that is not far from your home. One day, I sat in that cave and I wrote down my thoughts about my life and my career. I've never forgotten that cave. I'd like to be buried outside that cave. Will you take my body there tomorrow? Will you promise me that?'

And Fouqué promised.

———

Julien Sorel's last day was very peaceful. His head was full of beautiful thoughts.

The weather was warm and sunny. Julien enjoyed the fresh air as he walked to the guillotine.

'The world has never been so beautiful as it is today,' he thought.

Julien died simply. He did not need to impress any of the people who came to watch his execution. He did not make a speech. He did not throw money to the crowd. He was quiet and brave. And after his head was cut from his body, the three people who had loved him remembered their promises.

Mathilde de La Mole behaved like the lover of her famous ancestor. She was as strong as Marguerite of Navarre herself.

The day after Julien's execution, she visited Fouqué in the room where he had spent the night with his friend's body. Fouqué did not look up when Mathilde entered the room. He could not speak to her.

'I want to see him,' Mathilde said.

Fouqué pointed towards the blue coat which covered

Julien's body. He heard Mathilde lifting the coat and he heard her walking round the room.

When Fouqué looked up, he saw what Mathilde had done. Tears fell from his eyes. Mathilde had placed Julien's head on a small stone table. All around the table she had placed many lighted candles. She gently kissed Julien's forehead.

Fouqué kept his promise to Julien. The next day, Julien's body was carried to the little cave in the mountain and it was buried there. Mathilde de La Mole followed the procession in her carriage. She held her lover's head on her knees. When she reached the cave, she made a hole in the ground and she buried Julien's head.

———

A few months later, Mathilde bought some beautiful and expensive white stone from Italy. She paid some famous artists to decorate the cave with this stone.

Louise de Rênal tried to keep her promise to Julien too. She did not try to kill herself. But three days after Julien's execution, as she held her children in her arms, Louise died. Her great sadness had broken her heart.

Points for Understanding

1

Why did M. de Rênal want Sorel's son to teach his children? Give two reasons.

2

How did Julien impress: (a) Curé Chélan? (b) Louise de Rênal? (c) the mayor's children, his neighbours and servants?

3

1 Who has contempt for whom in this chapter? Why?
2 Who is jealous in this chapter? Why?

4

1 Describe these people and their characters: (a) Julien (b) the mayor of Verrières (c) Louise de Rênal (d) Mme Derville (e) Fouqué.
2 Give your opinion on these relationships: (a) Julien and M. de Rênal (b) Julien and Mme de Rênal.

5

1 How does a royal visitor to Verrières change Julien's life? Include these things in your answer: (a) an aristocrat (b) a guard of honour (c) a blessing
2 Why is this chapter given the title 'Passion and Guilt'?

6

1 Explain the meanings of these words: (a) *to trick, a trick*
  (b) *anonymous* (c) *secretly.*
2 Look at the events in this chapter and write three sentences using
  the words from (a), (b) and (c).

7

What decisions do these people make in this chapter? Why?
  (a) M. de Rênal (b) Élisa (c) Julien (d) Curé Chélan.

8

Is life difficult or easy for Julien at the seminary? Give reasons.

9

How does Julien use these things in this chapter? (a) the poems of
  Horace (b) a ladder.

10

What does Abbé Pirard tell Julien about these people? (a) the
  Marquis de La Mole (b) Norbert, the Comte de La Mole
  (c) Mathilde de La Mole.

11

Describe how the relationship between Julien and Mathilde has
  changed. Why has it changed?

12

Julien receives an invitation from Mathilde. (a) Why is he suspicious about their meeting? (b) What does he do?

13

The marquis says to Julien, 'I'm going to send you on an important mission.' What is Julien going to do?

14

What news does Julien hear when he returns to Paris?

15

There are three letters in this chapter. (a) Who asks for money and help? (b) Who tells secrets and betrays someone?

16

Why is Julien in a prison cell? What is going to happen to him?

17

1 These people visit Julien: Louise, Mathilde, Fouqué. (a) What does Julien ask each person to do? (b) What does each person do for Julien at the end?
2 Choose and give reasons. Julien Sorel is: (a) innocent and honest (b) dishonest and corrupt.

Glossary

1 **merchant ... diplomat** (page 4)
a *merchant* buys and sells goods. A *diplomat* is a government official who lives and works in another country.

2 **relationship** (page 4)
the way that two or more things or people are connected with each other. If two people make love, they have a *sexual relationship* with each other.

3 **quarrelled** – *to quarrel* (page 4)
an argument between two people who know each other well is a *quarrel*. People who are having an argument are *quarrelling*.

4 **priests** (page 4)
men who believe in God and teach people about the Catholic religion. *Priests* work in churches and help during religious ceremonies. Young men who want to be priests are trained in special schools called *seminaries*. Priests must not marry or have children. In France, the general name for a priest is *abbé*. A *curé* is a priest who helps in the church of a small town or village in France. More important priests are *bishops* and *archbishops*. The most important priest of the Catholic Church is the *Pope* who lives in Rome. Most priests wear black clothes. Some of the more important priests wear red clothes. During religious ceremonies, important priests wear long coats called *robes*.

5 **XVI** (page 4)
Roman numbers which are the symbols for the number 'sixteen'. X = 10, V = 5, I = 1. Louis XVI (SAY: Louis the Sixteenth) was the sixteenth king of France with the name Louis.

6 **tax** (page 5)
money that everyone has to pay to the government.

7 **aristocrats** (page 5)
men and woman from the highest social class. *Aristocrats* have power and a lot of money, land and property. French aristocrats have special titles, e.g. marquis, comte. See also pages 9 to 11.

8 **served** – *to serve* (page 5)
work for.

9 **high rank** (page 5)
a *rank* is a level or a position in an army. A soldier who has a *high rank* has an important position. e.g. major, colonel or general are high ranks.

10 **battles** (page 5)

fights between two armies during a war.

11 **honours** (page 5)

prizes such as land, money and property. *Honours* are usually given to people because they have done something which is brave or good. The *Cross of the Legion of Honour* was a prize given to Frenchmen who had pleased the king or his officials. It was a medal – a small flat piece of metal – in the shape of a cross. The medal was held on a small piece of coloured cloth.

12 **peasants** (page 5)

people who work on other people's farms. Some *peasants* work on their own small farms. This word is most often used about low-class people in poor countries, or people in history.

13 **traitor** – *to accuse someone of being a traitor* (page 6)

if you say that a someone has done something wrong, or that they have broken a law, you are *accusing* that person.

A *traitor* is a person who does something which makes trouble for their own country.

14 **executed** – *to be executed* (page 6)

be killed because you have broken an important law.

15 **Jacobins** (page 6)

the name of a group of people who first met together during the French Revolution (1789). The *Jacobins* believed that France should not have a king. They wanted many changes in the laws and government of France. Jacobins told the peasants not to obey the landowners. The leader of the Jacobins was Maximilien Robespierre. He was executed in 1794 and the Jacobins lost power.

16 **guillotines** (page 6)

machines that were used to cut off people's heads.

17 **protect** (page 7)

make sure that someone is not upset, or hurt, or in danger. Napoleon's soldiers fought France's enemies and made sure that its people were safe. They *protected* the country and its people.

18 **Ultras** (page 7)

After the French Revolution, a group of people who lived near the Jura Mountains met together. Members of the group were called *Ultras*. Their name came from the word, 'Ultramontanism' which means 'beyond the mountains'.

The Ultras believed that the Catholic Church in France should be completely controlled by the Pope in Rome.

19 *spy* (page 7)

someone who finds out secret information about a country or an organization. If you work as a *spy* you are *spying*. Someone who secretly watches another person is *spying on* that person.

20 **dishonesty and corruption** (page 8)

a *dishonest* person does not tell the truth and may steal things. *Corruption* is when a powerful person is dishonest, or breaks the law. A *corrupt* person might receive money for breaking a law or telling a secret.

21 **buried** – *to bury* (page 8)

when someone dies, their body is *buried*. It is put into the ground. Before the body is buried, a priest says some words in a ceremony called a *funeral*. The dead person's body might be buried in a place called a *tomb*. Tombs are made of stone.

22 **border** (page 12)

the official line between two countires.

23 **sawmills** (page 12)

buildings where timber (wood) from trees is cut into pieces by sharp blades which are called *saws*.

24 **Liberals** (page 13)

Liberals wanted changes to be made in France. And they wanted to change the way that the king ruled France. Liberals did not want aristocrats to have all the powerful positions in the government. They did not want the Church to tell people what to think and how to pray. They wanted more people to keep the money that they earned. Liberals wanted people to be able to make decisions about their own lives.

25 **respected** – *to be respected* (page 13)

if someone is *respected* people like them and think well of them. You *respect* someone because they are intelligent, or important. Or you respect them because they are kind and behave well. If you *show respect* to someone, you are very polite to them because you think that they are clever or important.

26 **impress** (page 13)

make people like you and think well of you. People might be *impressed by* you because you are clever, or rich, or polite. Or they might be *impressed with* your work or your behaviour.

27 **make deals with** (page 13)

a *deal* is an agreement, especially a business agreement. When two people *make a deal*, they agree on a price for something.

28 **theology** (page 14)
the study of God and religion.

29 **Latin** (page 16)
the language that the people of Rome spoke and wrote more than two thousand years ago.

30 **bad-mannered** (page 16)
a *bad-mannered* person behaves badly and is not polite. A person with *good manners* is polite and knows how to behave well.

31 **admired** – *to admire* (page 16)
if you like the way that someone looks, works, or behaves, you *admire* that person. You are that person's *admirer*. The feeling you have is *admiration*.

32 **careers** (page 16)
jobs that people are trained to do. They do the same work for most of their lives. e.g. Doctors are trained for a *career* in medicine.

33 **started to notice** – *to start to notice* (page 17)
if you see someone and suddenly think that they are now more interesting or attractive, you *start to notice* them. If you know that something is happening and you do nothing, you *take no notice of it*. If someone is near you, but you do not look at them, you *take no notice of them*.

34 **pretended** – *to pretend* (page 17)
the way that you speak or behave so that people believe that something is true, when it is not.

35 **scholar** (page 18)
a person who studies a particular subject and knows a lot about it. e.g. A *scholar* of Latin studies the language and knows it well.

36 **hero** (page 18)
someone who has done something very brave is a *hero*. If you like someone because of the things that they have done, that person is *your hero*.

37 **learned by heart** – *to learn by heart* (page 19)
read a text, or be told something, and then remember every word that you have read or heard.

38 **punish** (page 19)
do something to someone because they have done something wrong. A *punishment* is the way that someone is *punished*. e.g. The person might have to go to prison, or pay some money. These are punishments.

39 *find the courage* (page 20)

be able to do something although you know that it is dangerous or very difficult.

A frightened person, who behaves bravely, has *found courage.*

40 **complain** (page 22)

if you speak about something that is wrong and say that you are unhappy about it, you are *complaining.*

When a person goes to a second person and says that a third person has done something wrong, the first person is *making a complaint* about the third person.

41 **sincerity** (page 22)

an honest way of behaving that shows you really mean what you say or do.

42 **opinions** (page 22)

thoughts about someone or something. When someone *asks for your opinion*, they are asking to hear your thoughts about that thing.

43 **tailor** (page 22)

a person who makes and repairs clothes.

44 **knowledge** – *to test someone's knowledge* (page 23)

ask questions to find out if someone has learnt their lessons well.

45 **recited** – *to recite* (page 23)

repeat every word correctly.

46 **confident** (page 24)

not feel nervous or frightened. If you believe that you are right and you are behaving correctly, you are *confident.* Someone behaves *confidently*, or *with confidence*, because they are not worried.

47 **adored** – *to adore* (page 24)

love someone very much. *Adoration* is the strong feeling of love that you have for someone.

48 **scornful** (page 24)

if you think that someone is stupid, or wrong, you are *scornful* when you speak about them. Your words and your face show your *scorn* for that person or thing.

49 **contempt** – *to treat with contempt* (page 24)

contempt is when you have a strong feeling that someone (or something) is not important. If a person (or thing) is not good enough, you *treat them* (or it) *with contempt.* Because you think that they are unimportant, you show these feelings very strongly.

50 **resentful** (page 26)

a *resentful* person is angry with someone who has said or done something which has upset them.

51 **jealous** – to *be jealous* (page 26)

if someone has something that you want, or does something that you want to do, you are *jealous*. *Jealousy* is this feeling of sadness and anger.

52 **change his mind** (page 27)

if you have an idea and then decide to do something different, you have *changed your mind*.

53 **country** (page 29)

the land outside towns and cities is called the *countryside*. This word is often shortened to – the *country*.

54 **butterflies** (page 30)

insects with large colourful wings.

55 **mistress** (page 30)

a woman who is having a love affair – a sexual relationship – with a man. (See also Glossary 2.)

56 **prefer** (page 30)

like one thing more than another thing.

57 **shown any interest** – to *show interest* (page 30)

if you like somone very much and you let the person know this, you are *showing interest* in them.

58 **seduce** (page 30)

do or say things to someone so that they will have sex with you.

59 **revenge** – to *take revenge on someone* (page 30)

do something bad to someone because they have hurt you, or made you very unhappy.

60 **betray** (page 31)

when you know that you have done something that harms your country, family or friends, etc. you have *betrayed* them.

61 **mattresses** (page 33)

thick soft parts of beds.

62 **relieved** – to *be relieved* (page 35)

a feeling of happiness because a bad thing has not happened to you.

63 **passion and guilt** (page 38)

passion is an extremely strong feeling of love.

Guilt is the very strong feeling that you have when you know that you have done something wrong.

When someone breaks a law, they are taken to a court of law. The members of the court decide if the person has broken the law. If the court decides that the person did break the law, the person is *guilty*.

64 **equal** (page 38)

if a person's wealth, education and place in society is the same as your own, they are your *equal*. Julien is a poor peasant. But he knows that he is more intelligent and better educated than the mayor, who is middle-class. So Julien believes that Rênal should *treat him as his equal*.

65 **warn** (page 40)

if you tell someone that they are in danger, or that they must not do something, you are *warning* them not to do that thing. Your words are a *warning*.

66 **accompanied by** – *to be accompanied* (page 40)

when someone goes with you to all the places that you visit, you are *accompanied by* this person. A person who stays with someone for a long time is a *companion*.

67 **ancestors** (page 40)

members of your family who lived a long time ago.

68 **guard of honour** (page 41)

a group of soldiers who make sure that their leader is safe during a special ceremony.

69 **borrowed** – *to borrow* (page 41)

use something that is owned by someone else.

70 **spurs and sword** (page 41)

spurs are short pieces of metal that someone wears on the heels of their boots while they are riding a horse. When the rider touches the horse with the spurs, the horse will move faster. A *sword* was a long sharp metal weapon that was used by soldiers.

71 **arrogant** (page 41)

an *arrogant person* thinks that they are better or more important than other people. Arrogant people often do not behave politely towards other people.

72 **Monseigneur the Bishop** (page 43)

the correct title for a bishop of the Catholic Church in France.

73 **blessing** (page 43)

a sign made by religious person. The bishop makes a shape of a cross in the air in front of the people. He then asks God to keep them safe and well.

74 **blamed** – *to blame* (page 44)
you *blame* a person who makes trouble for you. If you *take the blame*, you are saying that you made the problem.

75 **adultery** (page 44)
if a man and a woman have a sexual relationship and one of them is married, they are *committing adultery*. One law of the Christian church says that adultery is very bad – it is a *sin*.

76 **unfaithful** (page 44)
if you have a sexual relationship with someone who is not your husband, or wife, or partner, you are being *unfaithful*.

77 **monastery** (page 45)
a building where priests live, work and pray.

78 **glue** (page 48)
a substance which sticks two things together. Two piece of paper can be *glued* together.

79 **threaten** (page 48)
promise to make trouble for someone or hurt them.

80 **dismissed** – *to dismiss someone* (page 48)
send someone away from their work forever.

81 **insulted my honour** – *to insult someone's honour* (page 49)
an old-fashioned phrase which not often used today. Louise de Rênal is saying: 'I would never make love with any man except my husband. I am a good wife. Anyone who says that I have a lover is lying. These people are insulting me – they're saying I'm a bad woman.' Of course, we know that this is not the truth. Louise is saying this to trick Rênal. She wants to stop people talking about her relationship with Julien.

82 **suspiciously** (page 49)
if you think that someone has done something wrong, but you are not sure, you are *suspicious of* that person. You *suspect* that person of doing something. That person is a *suspect*.

83 **destroyed** – *to destroy* (page 53)
when something terrible happens and people's lives are changed forever, their lives are *destroyed*. Someone's happiness can *be destroyed* if another person is cruel to them, or takes everything away from them. If a thing is broken completely, it is destroyed.

84 **contradicted each other** – *to contradict* (page 58)

say the opposite of someone else's ideas or words about a thing, but also say that your words are correct. If two or more ideas (or stories) about the same subject have a difference in them, that difference is a *contradiction*.

85 **cell** (page 59)

a priest's small room in a seminary or a monastery. (See Glossaries 4 and 77.) *Cell* is also the word for a small room in a prison.

86 **Jesuits** (page 60)

members of a religious organization – the Society of Jesus – which was started in 1540 by Ignatius Loyola.

Jesuits closely followed the laws of the Catholic Church which was ruled by the Pope in Rome. Jesuits held great power in Europe between the end of the sixteenth century and the beginning of the seventeenth century. Jesuits were known for teaching and studying Christianity.

At the time of this story, the Jesuits had powerful positions in the Church and the government in France. They also controlled many of the seminaries in France. (See Glossary 4.)

87 **Jansenists** (page 60)

a group of people who agreed with the ideas of a Dutchman called Cornelius Jansen (1585–1638). *Jansenists* believed in the laws of the Catholic Church but they did not accept the rule of the Pope. Jansenists were the enemies of the Jesuits. (See Glossary 86.)

88 **cathedral** (page 60)

a very large, important church. A *cathedral* is usually made of stone and has beautiful decorations.

89 **festival** (page 60)

a day or a time when there is a holiday. *Festivals* often take place at the same time as a special religious ceremony.

90 **procession** (page 61)

a group of people who move in a slow line during a ceremony.

91 **ladders** (page 61)

you use a *ladder* to reach a high place. It is made of two long pieces of wood or metal that are joined by small pieces called rungs.

92 **resign** (page 63)

tell your employer that you are leaving your job. You give this information to your employer in a *letter of resignation*.

93 **trust** (page 71)

believe that someone is honest, kind and helpful. If you believe that someone will say or do something which will hurt you, you *do not trust them*. You *distrust* that person.

94 **mocked** – *to mock* (page 77)

say something which shows that you think someone or something is stupid or foolish.

95 **Grand Passion** (page 79)

when someone deeply loves another person but they can never be with them, or marry them – this is a *Grand Passion*.

96 **arrested** – *to be arrested* (page 80)

if the police *arrest* someone, they take the person to a police station because they believe the person has broken a law.

97 **prove** (page 83)

find something which shows that your words or thoughts were true. The things that you find are *proofs*.

98 **mission** (page 87)

a special job or special work.

99 **crime** (page 104)

a *crime* is when you do something which breaks a law. e.g. Stealing and murder are crimes.

100 **gaoler** (page 104)

a person who works in a prison and guards the prisoners.

101 **bribed** – *to bribe* (page 105)

give money to someone so that they will help you. The money is a *bribe*. *Bribery* is wrong. Both the person who takes the bribe and the person who offers the bribe are breaking the law.

Dictionary extracts adapted from the Macmillan English Dictionary © Bloomsbury Publishing Plc 2002 and © A & C Black Publishers Ltd 2005.

Macmillan Education
4 Crinan Street
London N1 9XW
A division of Macmillan Publishers Limited
Companies and representatives throughout the world

ISBN 978–1–4050–7458–2

This version of *The Red and the Black* by Stendhal was retold by
F. H. Cornish for Macmillan Readers
First published by Macmillan 2007
Text © Macmillan Publishers Limited 2007
Design and illustration © Macmillan Publishers Limited 2007
This version first published 2007

Illustrated by Mike Lacey
Cover by Bridgeman Art Library

Printed and bound by Ashford Colour Press Ltd.

2018 2017
12 11 10 9 8 7